797,885 Books
are available to read at

Forgotten Books

www.ForgottenBooks.com

Forgotten Books' App
Available for mobile, tablet & eReader

ISBN 978-1-330-99293-7
PIBN 10130894

This book is a reproduction of an important historical work. Forgotten Books uses state-of-the-art technology to digitally reconstruct the work, preserving the original format whilst repairing imperfections present in the aged copy. In rare cases, an imperfection in the original, such as a blemish or missing page, may be replicated in our edition. We do, however, repair the vast majority of imperfections successfully; any imperfections that remain are intentionally left to preserve the state of such historical works.

Forgotten Books is a registered trademark of FB &c Ltd.
Copyright © 2015 FB &c Ltd.
FB &c Ltd, Dalton House, 60 Windsor Avenue, London, SW19 2RR.
Company number 08720141. Registered in England and Wales.

For support please visit www.forgottenbooks.com

1 MONTH OF FREE READING

at

www.ForgottenBooks.com

By purchasing this book you are eligible for one month membership to ForgottenBooks.com, giving you unlimited access to our entire collection of over 700,000 titles via our web site and mobile apps.

To claim your free month visit:

www.forgottenbooks.com/free130894

* Offer is valid for 45 days from date of purchase. Terms and conditions apply.

Similar Books Are Available from
www.forgottenbooks.com

The Little Boss
A Comedy Drama in Four Acts, by Frank L. Bixby

The Ratnavali
A Sanskrit Drama, by Harṣavardhana Srīsachandra Chakravartī

A Scout's Honor
A Play for Boys in One Act, by Clifton Lisle

Shakspere's Holinshed
The Chronicle and the Historical Plays Compared, by W. G. Boswell Stone

Three Plays for Puritans
Being the Third Volume of His Collected Plays, by Bernard Shaw

Sleepy Hollow
A Romance of the Revolution in Three Acts, by George M. Rosener

A Study of the Drama
by Brander Matthews

A Treasury of Plays for Children
by Montrose Jonas Moses

Napoleon
A Play, by Herbert Trench

Mice and Men, A Romantic Comedy in Four Acts
by Madeleine Lucette Ryley

Five One Act Plays
by Stanley Houghton

Freytag's Technique of the Drama
An Exposition of Dramatic Composition and Art, by Gustav Freytag

The Importance of Being Earnest
A Trivial Comedy for Serious People, by Oscar Wilde

The Melting-Pot
Drama in Four Acts, by Israel Zangwill

The Best Plays of 1920-1921
by John Arthur Chapman

Selected Dramas of John Dryden
With the Rehearsal, by George Villiers

Six Dramas of Calderón
by Calderón De La Barca

The Chinese Drama
by William Stanton

Robespierre
A Lyrical Drama, by R. H. Patterson

The Plays of Moliere, Vol. 1
by Molière

An impression of Mrs. Fiske by Ernest Haskel

MRS. FISKE

HER VIEWS ON ACTORS, ACTING,
AND THE PROBLEMS
OF PRODUCTION

RECORDED BY
ALEXANDER WOOLCOTT

WITH PHOTOGRAPHS

NEW YORK
THE CENTURY CO.
1917

Copyright, 1917, by
THE CENTURY CO.

Published, October, 1917

CONTENTS

CHAPTER		PAGE
I	An Assault on the Repertory Idea	3
II	On Ibsen the Popular	41
III	To the Actor in the Making	75
IV	A Theater in Spain	108
V	Going to the Play	145
VI	Postscript	185
VII	Marie Augusta Davey	199

LIST OF ILLUSTRATIONS

	PAGE
An impression of Mrs. Fiske by Ernest Haskel	*Frontispiece*
Portrait of Mrs. Fiske	5
Mrs. Fiske as *Tess*	16
Mrs. Fiske as *Becky Sharp*	26
Charles Waldron and Mrs. Fiske in the first scene of Edward Sheldon's "The High Road"	35
Mrs. Fiske as *Hedda*	46
"Mr. Fiske has been my artistic backbone . . ."	55
A typical page from Mrs. Fiske's prompt copy of an Ibsen play	65
The confession scene from "Erstwhile Susan"	71
Mrs. Fiske as *Rebecca West* in "Rosmersholm"	78
Mrs. Fiske—1917	91
Mrs. Fiske as *Gilberti* in "Frou-Frou"	102
Salvation Nell	111
Minnie Maddern Fiske	121
The first act of "Salvation Nell" (1908)	131
Becky Sharp	142

ILLUSTRATIONS

"Erstwhile Susan" . . . .
"When I remember Duse. . . . .
"Mary of Magdala" . . . . .
Mrs. Fiske as *Tess* . . . .
Mrs. Fiske as *Hannele* . . . . . .
Mrs. Fiske at four . . . .
Minnie Maddern at sixteen . . . . .
An early folder . . . .
Minnie Maddern shortly before her retirement from the stage . . . .

MRS. FISKE

MRS. FISKE

I

AN ASSAULT ON THE REPERTORY IDEA

*H*EDDA GABLER sat just across the table from me at supper after the play. It was all very well for Grant Allen in his day to say that *Hedda* was "nothing more or less than the girl we take down to dinner in London nineteen times out of twenty." Certainly she was something more this time, for *Tess of the D'Urbervilles*—not Hardy's *Tess*, perhaps, but ours—sat there, too. I was at supper with *Hedda* and *Tess* and *Becky Sharp*, but surely that was *Becky's* red hair that could be glimpsed in the shadow of the big hat and voluminous veil. That erect figure, vital, alert, indefatigable, eloquently animate, surely that was *Becky*. There was something of *Becky*, also, in the mutinous, gleaming humor,

MRS. FISKE

and a little something of *Cynthia Karslake*, stepping forth briskly from the pages of Langdon Mitchell's glittering comedy. Then there was my dear friend *Mrs. Bumpstead-Leigh*, or at least her unmistakable lorgnette, not wielded now for the abashed discomfiture of others, but flirted and brandished, like the fan and the morsel of a handkerchief, just to enforce a few of the more fervent gestures—those vivid, arresting gestures which so emphasize and underscore a speech that, when you wish to repeat it in black and white, you must needs out-Brisbane Brisbane in your desperate recourse to capitals or italics. In the utter self-effacement of these enthusiasms of opinion, as we talked of the theater, there were the accents of great *Lona Hessel*, and in the deep conviction, the all-persuasive conviction, something of *Rebecca West* and *Salvation Nell*, sweet *Nell* of old Cherry Hill. It was not merely that you could not choose but hear: you could not choose but believe. She could say "Bosh!" for instance, with simply devastating effect. In fact, she did.

"Bosh!" said Mrs. Fiske, for of course it *was* Mrs. Fiske, "do not talk to me about the

Portrait of Mrs. Fiske

THE REPERTORY IDEA

repertory idea. It is an outworn, needless, impossible, *harmful* scheme."

"I gather," I answered brightly, "that you are opposed to repertory."

"I am, I am indeed. In all my days in the theater I have never encountered such a preposterous will-o'-the-wisp. This, my friend, is an age of specialization, and in such an age the repertory theater is an anachronism, a ludicrous anachronism."

"But Mr. Granville Barker—and he is really a great man—"

"Ah, yes," she assented cheerfully, and yet with a faintly perceptible undertone of reservation in her voice.

"Well, Mr. Barker not only carried out the repertory idea in his season at Wallack's, but admitted then that he could conceive of no other kind of theater."

"Exactly," said Mrs. Fiske, in triumph. Indeed, she quite pounced on Mr. Barker and on me. I suspect she had been waiting for us. "And let me tell you that nothing more harmful has happened in the American theater in *years* than the Barker season at Wallack's."

Harmful? One heard many unkind things

said of Mr. Barker at the time, but there never had been the suggestion that he worked an evil spell. Those who rejoiced over his "Man with a Dumb Wife" never suspected him later of doing harm in the theater.

"Harmful," said Mrs. Fiske—"harmful and pernicious. One play, 'Androcles and the Lion,' Mr. Barker produced perfectly. It was a beautiful achievement, and what followed was all the more tragic because he had already shown himself a master of his art. A master. He had shown us how splendidly he could shine as a producer if only he would be a specialist—a specialist like several of our own, though of the greatest value to us all because the loftier literature of the theater would have no terrors for Granville Barker. But he put the same company through the paces of a quite different play for which it was grotesquely unfitted. That is the essence and the evil of the repertory idea. He slaughtered 'The Doctor's Dilemma'—slaughtered a capital play before our very eyes beyond all hope of a resuscitation in this generation."

In particular, as she recalled that evening, Mrs. Fiske saw the beautiful rôle of the wife

THE REPERTORY IDEA

so atrociously played that she wanted to rush from the theater and forget that it had ever happened. And what specially depressed her was the evidence of the very harm she feared having its deadly effect on her own ingenuous companion, an earnest "student of the drama," who was applauding conscientiously at the end of each act.

"Why the applause?" asked Mrs. Fiske, coldly, and when her awestruck guest murmured something about Granville Barker, it was more than she could bear. She had told me this much when she paused, as if amused and a little scandalized by one of her own memories. But what her reply had been there is no telling now, for she wanted to explain clearly just why she felt that Mr. Barker's activities had worked "direct mischief."

"Mr. Barker's unfortunate influence was the direct result, you see, of the importance of his position, of the fact that he was supposed to stand for what was *good* in the theater. When an ordinary manager"—she named one, but the reader can fill in to suit himself, for the range of choice is large—"when an ordinary manager produces a play badly, even very badly, he

MRS. FISKE

works no great harm. He has made no pretensions to what is idealistic in the theater We have not taken him seriously. But Mr. Barker is *not* an ordinary manager. When he opened the doors of Wallack's the public was invited to come and see something fine and true, something representative of the best. We were told that here was something at least approaching the realization of a certain ideal. We were told that we should be safe in regarding the offerings of the Barker system as offerings in good art, things real, vital, progressive; things to set the intellectual pace; something like a standard, a model, something to measure by.

"Now, all of us who know the theater know that even the most highly intelligent and cultivated people are for the most part mere children there. People whose understanding and taste in literature, painting, and music are beyond question are, for the most part, ignorant of what is good or bad art in the theater. This is strange, but true; and it always has been true. I shall never forget the first time I saw Duse in 'La Locandiera.'" Mrs. Fiske's eyes shone as they always shine when she names the greatest lady of them all. "There, my friend,

THE REPERTORY IDEA

was probably the most perfect and utterly beautiful example of delicate comedy in all the world of acting in our day, yet I saw the performance in the company of a highly cultivated woman who was excessively bored and who missed completely the marvelous spirit and the astounding revelation of technical fluency in that matchless performance."

"But 'The Doctor's Dilemma,'" I ventured.

"Why," said Mrs. Fiske, "the public, always so easily misled in the theater, had been led this time to believe the Barker production good art, whereas in truth it was bad art, very bad. That several of the parts were beautifully acted could not for a moment excuse the fact that, considered as a whole, the performance was *atrocious*. Yet how could it be otherwise when the two leading parts, *Jennifer Dubedat* and the title rôle, were completely misrepresented? Furthermore, entire scenes in the play were out of key and out of tempo. Now what should we say of an opera in which the leading rôles were abominably sung and in which whole passages were out of key and out of tempo? Your audience, trained to music, would immediately recognize the extraordinary deficiency and condemn it. In the case of 'The Doctor's Dilemma,' however, the audience, for the most part untrained in dramatic criticism, accepted as an example of good art the misrepresentation, the *mutilation* of a splendid play. So the mischief was worked, and, because of the very conspicuousness of Mr. Barker, ignorance and bad taste were encouraged. For Mr. Barker was more than an ordinary manager: he was a *movement*. And I have never known a 'movement' in the theater that did not work direct and serious harm. Indeed, I have sometimes felt that the very people associated with various 'uplifting' activities in the theater are people who are *astoundingly* lacking in idealism."

I could not help luxuriating then in the thought of certain very vocal persons overhearing that remark. But we were not done with Mr. Barker.

"He was a movement," I prompted.

"But how many knew he was a movement in the wrong direction?"

There was the point. How many knew? We were agreed, then, that all growth in the theater is just progress in the recognition of

THE REPERTORY IDEA

what is good and what is bad, of what is right and what is wrong—the recognition by the playgoers, that is, as well as by the workers on the other side of the footlights. It is the slow upbuilding of a public for good art.

"So you see, my friend, we have had nothing so harmful and pernicious befall our theater in years as Granville Barker's season—unless—" and here Mrs. Fiske resorted to the whisper used by those in imminent danger of being shot for treason—"unless it was the New Theater."

This was a leap; and yet it was natural to move from the sorry, dismantled Wallack's to the sumptuous temple that overlooks Central Park from the west, the mausoleum which sheltered at first and for a little time the most ambitious attempt to endow drama ever made in America. It is no longer the temple of the drama, but the temple of the chorus girl. The New Theater has become a music hall.

"Whatever the fine idealism, the unselfishness, the splendid and genuine philanthropy that launched the New Theater," said Mrs. Fiske, "it was headed from the first for shipwreck."

MRS. FISKE

"Even had the building been right and the people within it right?"

"Even then," she went on. "There was one factor bound to wreck it."

"And that one factor—"

"Repertory."

This is worth underscoring, because there is little reason to believe that many of those who benevolently launched the New Theater yet recognize this diagnosis of the ills of which that endeavor perished. It is certain that four years after the New Theater closed its doors these same men were ready to endow virtually the same scheme under the directorship of Mr. Barker, the great producer from overseas. It is equally certain that even after Mr. Barker's first season they were ready to establish him here, and it should be kept in mind that this project failed of fulfilment for entirely adventitious and personal reasons. It would be neither tactful nor chivalrous to set these forth at this time. Besides, it does not matter. It is important to remember only that if Mr. Barker is not now the head of a lavishly endowed theater in New York, it is not because of any recognized flaws in his theory of the

Mrs. Fiske as *Tess*

THE REPERTORY IDEA

theater. And his theory of the theater is repertory. That theory is apparently still in favor. You are sure to hear it expounded at every luncheon given by the Society for the Gracious Patronage of the Drama. The very word is one to conjure with among all the little putterers in the theater.

They dream of an American Comédie Française. They yearn for an institutional playhouse which shall have a fairly fixed company for alternating performances of good plays, that shall provide change and freshness and much experience for the actor, while it gives deserved, but unexpected, longevity to masterpieces too frail and precious, perhaps, to fill the auditorium eight times a week, and yet well worth nursing along in repertory. This was the theory of the New Theater; this is Mr. Barker's theory of the theater. It is not Mrs. Fiske's.

Her heretical and quite unfashionable sentiments on the subject were expressed over the supper-table one snowy evening. It was after the performance of "Erstwhile Susan" at a theater "somewhere in the United States," and this is only the memory of that conversation. From such memories alone—mine and others'—is there any prospect of spreading before the reader her theory of the theater; for in all the years she has worked in it she has written no solemn treatises, spoken seldom, given forth few, if any, interviews, and, having precious little enthusiasm for the past, indulged in no reminiscences. This has probably been due to no settled policy of stately silence, but rather to the overwhelming impulse of evasion every time an opportunity has arisen. It has been due a little, I imagine, to a feeling that as long as she would stage and play a piece, no more could be asked of her; a little, too, to her alert consciousness of the absurd, her lively horror of seeming to take herself too seriously. There it is—the deep-seated aversion to appearing in any degree oracular. Some time ago, as a matter of fact, there had been a vague suggestion of a dignified outgiving in which I was to conspire; but by the time I reached the place appointed the impulse had passed and left merely a disarming, but impenetrable, smile.

"Who am I, to talk about the theater?" she asked that time, quite as though I had suggested

THE REPERTORY IDEA

it. "How can I, who in twenty years have done upon the stage so much of which I cannot approve, speak now as producer, as stage-dircetor, or as actress? Ah, but the saving grace is that Mr. Fiske and I have made no pretensions, though it is maddeningly true in the theater that because you do a thing people will insist on assuming that you *vouch* for it. Why, I have occasionally acted in plays that I could not possibly respect—played night after night, too, when every night to go to the theater was a wearing, aging task. Of course I should have refused to go on. I should have. That would have been the *right* thing to do. I should have sailed out of the stifling theater, head up and free. I thought, to be sure, that each time I had good reasons for going on; but," she added ruefully, "I dare say there never *is* a good reason for doing wrong."

"Of course," she resumed, with more cheerfulness, "while it is quite out of the question to speak as actress or producer,—I place no false estimate on my career in those capacities,—I might say something as a dramatic critic. I think I am a *safe* critic, and in my time have been a bit of a playgoer myself. But, no,"—

this with a dismaying access of firmness,—"after all, there is nothing to talk about."

Thus ended that project, and thus, I rather imagine, has ended many another earlier projcet of the same nature. Mrs. Fiske's theory of the theater, then, must be gathered largely from the memories of unguarded conversations —such memories as these.

So this—one of several I must recall and put on paper for the reader—was a conversation across a platter that contained, as I remember, an omelet, which refection and the repertory idea we proceeded to demolish at some length and with great gusto. We approved the former and were scornful of the latter as an impossible scheme, quite impossible.

"A lovely dream, perhaps?"

"A lovely dream that cannot come true. In the first place, no single company, even though it had years and years in which to prepare, could give five entirely different plays and give them all properly. By all the laws of chance a company suitable for one would destroy the other four. It is grandiose presumption to pretend that a repertory theater can compete ar-

THE REPERTORY IDEA

tistically with such a production as Mr. Belasco could make with a specially selected cast, such a production, by the way, as he came close to making for 'Marie Odile.' There were only two false notes in 'Marie Odile.' For the rest, an ideal was realized perfectly.

"And it is no easy task. Let me tell you that only once in twenty years have Mr. Fiske and I succeeded in achieving what to me was an absolutely *perfect* performance. Think of that—only once in twenty years! We have, I think, several times approached close to the ideal, as did Mr. Belasco with 'Marie Odile'; but only once has my own personal critical sense been completely satisfied in our own personal effort.

"That satisfaction came to me in our first production of 'Salvation Nell.' A distinguished critic at the time said that it was 'incredibly' well acted. He was right. I can hardly tell you what an effort it represented. I cannot *begin* to tell you how many times Mr. Fiske and I virtually dismissed an entire company; how over and over again members of the cast were weeded out and others engaged; how over and over again we would start with an al-

MRS. FISKE

most entirely new company, until every part, from Holbrook Blinn's down to the very tiniest, was perfectly realized; how much there was of private rehearsal; of the virtual opening of a dramatic conservatory; how much of the most exquisite care before 'Salvation Nell' was ready."

So you may guess that when Mrs. Fiske is out in the provinces and sees a play advertised to be given "with the original cast," she is a little taken aback. What? They have made no improvements since they began? And then, encouraged by the suspicion that the poster is mendacious from sheer force of habit, she throws off her fears and goes to the play.

"I think," she went on, "that 'Erstwhile Susan' is excellently done, and that we had *fairly* approached perfection in 'Leah Kleschna' and 'The New York Idea.' So far as the impression upon the public and the critics went, these last two were far more important achievements than 'Salvation Nell.'"

"At least," I agreed, "the impression of the acting in 'Kleschna' and the Mitchell comedy was far more brilliant. Certainly it was

THE REPERTORY IDEA

praised much more highly than the acting in 'Salvation Nell.'"

"Whereas," said Mrs. Fiske, "the truth is that in neither of them was the ideal in acting realized with such absolute perfection as it was in the play by Edward Sheldon. In each there was one tiny false note—a note the casual observer would never hear, that only the most astute critic would be aware of. Yet a production is either *right* or it is not, and for me these little false notes spoiled the ideal. The *ideal* was spoiled in 'The New York Idea,' where, nevertheless, you had Mr. Arliss playing a part that Mr. Mitchell had written expressly for him and that therefore fitted him as, in the ordinary course of events, he could not hope to be fitted again. Mr. Arliss was perfect. There was John Mason at his splendid best, and there was Marian Lea. Dear me, what weeks and months we spent persuading her to return to the stage just for this! And yet I should have to go far back to recall anything so exquisite in high comedy as Marian Lea's performance in her husband's glittering play.

"And by the way," she added, smiling, "right

MRS. FISKE

here is a very pretty illustration of the virtual impossibility of safety in this precious repertory system you are all so fond of. In 'The New York Idea' the only false note was sounded by an actor whose performance in 'Leah Kleschna' had been superb. Repertory, indeed!"

It was evident by this time that a producer must find for every play its own particular cast or die in the attempt. But even a company miraculously fitted to half a dozen plays would, she argued, scarcely be able to give half, let alone all, of them in a single season.

"To play an important new rôle in one play by Ibsen or by any of the great moderns would take an actor all of a year," Mrs. Fiske confessed. "I could not possibly do two in a season and do either of them well. And so it is with most of the players I know. I remember Mr. Arliss saying that it took him six months to perfect a part, but I suspect he was underestimating. I remember asking Madame Janauschek—*there* was a great actress, my friend, a heroic creature, the last of a race of giants—I asked *her* one day how long she needed to master a part, and she, who had had her training in the quick changes at the court

Mrs. Fiske as *Becky Sharp*

THE REPERTORY IDEA

theater, said that two months was the very *least* she must have. I simply cannot understand the hardihood of those who suggest that any company should undertake such a staggering program as the repertory advocates invariably propose."

You see, Mrs. Fiske is obdurate. Stories of repertory's success in Europe leave her unmoved. What may be good for France or Germany is not necessarily good for us. Perhaps, she will admit, it is more feasible in a country where a long-developed art sense is stronger among the playgoers, who can thereby discard what is bad and recognize immediately what is good, in a country where the theater itself has been subjected for generations to such a shaking-down and weeding-out process as we need so badly here.

"We need it, even though we lost ninety per cent. of our actors," said Mrs. Fiske, with the greatest cheerfulness. "Though, mind you, such a weeding-out should not be done too hastily."

And she told then the story of a charming genius who once played with her for a little time in "Becky Sharp." He never learned any of

MRS. FISKE

his lines, but he was entirely honorable about it, for by some mysterious system of his own he did manage to learn his cues, so that his fellow-players were not left stranded in the middle of a dialogue. At last it was necessary to give him notice, and this was no sooner served than he gave a performance so perfected and so striking that every audience was thrilled, and Mrs. Fiske herself fairly uplifted. And she had already engaged another actor for the part! It was too desolating.

"You see, we must not weed out too hastily. For example, they say William Gillette was quite too impossible when he first went upon the stage, yet it would have been a pity to have weeded *him* out."

Unabashed by the Continent, Mrs. Fiske will certainly not quail when the repertory enthusiast brandishes the Metropolitan to confound her. What may work well enough in the opera-house will not settle the more subtle and complex problems of the theater.

"Besides," she said, "there they have all the greatest artists of the world under one roof. I admit it might be rather interesting to see a repertory theater that boasted a Duse and an

THE REPERTORY IDEA

Irving and a Terry and a Réjane and a few more like them all in one great, flexible company. This company the opera has. They seem willing enough to endow opera on such a scale, but I take it that the most multitudinous Mæcenas—all Wall Street, no less—would not attempt to endow such a *theater*."

And, as I learned, it does no good to remind her of the repertory ventures with which she herself has been identified, notably, of course, in the first season of her return to the stage as Mrs. Fiske and then, years before, when she was a child in the middle West and would be drafted for the children's rôles if some such "visiting" star as John McCullough or Mary Anderson passed that way.

"And they thought nothing of giving a different play every night," she said, with a smile for the days of labor so titanic that if you even suggested the like to one of our actors to-day he would swoon. "But that was long ago, and I *told* you that repertory was outworn. Besides, I'm not aware any one ever pretended it was the *best* way, the artistic way. Then it was the only possible way. And, in any case," she added with perfect finality, "you can

29

scarcely expect me to approve my own career in the theater. I do *not* approve it."

Nor was she moved by a reminder that Mr. Irving and Miss Terry, or, for that matter, that Duse, had brought repertories of plays to this country.

"It is true," she said, "that Henry Irving would bring us a large repertory of noble plays, almost perfectly produced. But not one of them at first had its place in a repertory. Each was a highly specialized offering, each the result of months of concentrated thought, study, preparation, and development.

"Perhaps," she admitted, "your repertory theater *would* nurse along a fragile piece, but its effect on strong plays would be disastrous. Even if by some miracle they were played well, they would be played intermittently and comparatively seldom. Comparatively few would see them, and this process simply burns up the literature of the stage. Suppose that 'The Great Divide' had been done at the New Theater. Think of that!"

What I did think of was Charles Frohman's gallant experiment with the repertory idea in London, when, abetted by the same Granville

THE REPERTORY IDEA

Barker, he sank a king's ransom in the production of many fine plays, among them "Justice," which, for all its silken playing, knew only a dozen performances and did not come into its own until a specialist gave Galsworthy his due five years later in New York.

"But badly played," Mrs. Fiske resumed, after this interruption, "such plays are simply slaughtered. Like the poor 'Doctor's Dilemma.' Or like Masefield's 'Tragedy of Nan,' which demands the most subtle treatment, and Arnold Bennett's 'The Honeymoon,' each of which the Stage Society killed in a single night. That exquisite little play of Mr. Bennett's had been close to my heart for a long time. For years Mr. Fiske and I searched in vain for just the right actor to play the part of the aviator. We searched for him in this country and we searched for him in England. When we found him, it was our intention to secure the play, if possible, and to produce it. But we never found the ideal actor for the part. And so a plan which I had greatly cherished had to be abandoned.

"But the Stage Society had no hesitancy in the matter of casting this delicate play—this play that could be crushed as easily as the wings of a butterfly. Thus was the lovely 'Honeymoon' killed and thrown away."

So a comedy that, with a brilliant Belasco production, might have flourished like the green bay-tree or "The Boomerang," was simply destroyed. Yet it did seem a little unfair to the already sorely beset repertory idea to make it shoulder the sins of such audible, but vague and ineffectual, idealists as the Stage Society and its like.

"Perhaps it *is* unfair," Mrs. Fiske agreed reluctantly, "and yet it seems all of a piece to me. The itch of the vague idealist to get his, or more often *her*, hands on the theater, sometimes, I suspect, just the long-thwarted ambition of the stage-struck girl to get behind the scenes, invariably takes the form of a demand for repertory. It always *has* taken this form, even back to the days when I was a girl and there was a great clatter about the Theater of Arts and Letters. The uplift societies are never content to destroy *one* play; they must needs destroy three or four.

"These enthusiasts all cry out the while for the perfect thing in the theater, quite regardless

THE REPERTORY IDEA

of the fact that we have had it often, or at least come as close to it from time to time as in my opinion we ever shall. Mr. Palmer, Mr. Daly, Mr. Belasco many times closely approached the ideal. And what an illumination and inspiration such an approach is! How it uplifts and educates! To the actor in the making what a solid *help* it is! The opportunity merely to witness one perfect performance would give him more of strength and guidance than would his own playing of twenty parts in more or less imperfect productions. He could see such performances at such a national theater as we might have if—but that is another story. We'll come back to it one of these days.

"And, after all, the disposition of the more clamorous repertory enthusiasts to ignore these achievements is merely irritating. My real objection to their theory of the theater is that it is destructive of valuable theatrical property. That is it: *it destroys property.*"

Whereupon I retreated hastily, and attempted to consolidate my position on that last firm stand the defenders of repertory always take, the good of the actor. Now, one who will admit that repertory is unnecessary in such a

MRS. FISKE

city as New York, which, with its great variety of plays, is itself a repertory theater; who will admit that no one company can hope to embody perfectly the marked divergences of several modern plays; that that author is best served who has the whole wide world to draw on for each specialized cast, will still cling to the scheme in behalf of the actor. Winthrop Ames, emerging from the wreck of the New Theater, can see this one excuse for repertory, the actor's interest. Does it not stunt the actor's growth to play one rôle month after month, maybe year after year? Surely you remember that moment in the recent Follies where the bogus Jane Cowl chokes back her sobs long enough to give voice to the actor's lament: "They gave me a crying part in 'Within the Law,' and oh, my God, it was a *success!*" For freshness, change, experience, does not the actor need the shifting programs of the repertory theater? Else how shall we train the Duses, the Irvings, the Mrs. Fiskes, the Forbes-Robertsons of 1930?

"Is it not necessary, then, for the training of the actor?"

Mrs. Fiske laughed immoderately.

"To educate the actor at the expense of the

Charles Waldron and Mrs. Fiske in the first scene of Edward Sheldon's "The High Road"

THE REPERTORY IDEA

public and dramatic literature!" she exclaimed in great amusement. "Bless you, that will *never* do. It might be fairly safe if they would say: 'Here we are giving imperfect and inadequate performances. They are not good art, but they will help train our actors.' Not that I am sure it would train them, mind you, and I am quite certain it's a needless extravagance.

"I do not know who started the precious notion that an actor needs half a dozen parts a season in order to develop his art. Some very lazy fellow, I suspect. If he has *one* rôle that amounts to anything, that has some substance and inspiration, he simply cannot exhaust its possibilities in less than a year. He cannot. Probably he cannot even play it perfectly for the first time before the end of the first season. And if his parts are empty and unnourishing, I cannot for the life of me see how the mere fact of having six instead of one in a season will avail him anything. Then suppose the director is incompetent. Directors usually are, you know. And, under incompetent direction, is not your actor in the making better off if he need play only one part badly rather than six parts badly?"

MRS. FISKE

Then how is the young actor to be trained? Mrs. Fiske is not entirely obdurate against the provincial stock companies, and yet she is a little afraid of them. They might serve their purpose in the young actor's apprenticeship if, advised by her, he would keep reminding himself: "This is all wrong, wrong, wrong. I cannot play *Smith* while I am memorizing *Brown*. This does not teach me acting. It teaches me tricks. I am getting a certain ease and facility, but it is all *wrong*."

But will he keep this in mind? Will he not rather gain confidence and nothing else? She shudders at the consequences which she has seen so often.

"He starts with the firm touch on the wrong note, and as he grows more and more confident, the touch becomes firmer and firmer. To our great dismay, the false step is taken then with a new and disconcerting air of sureness and authority. In all the theater, my friend, there is nothing quite so deadly as this firmer and firmer touch on the wrong note."

So suppose he accepts an engagement in New York and has just one part that lasts and lasts and lasts. I wanted to know about him.

THE REPERTORY IDEA

"If at the end of the season he has exhausted it," Mrs. Fiske advised, "let him resist all inducements to continue. And if during that first season his part does not stimulate, nourish, and tax him, let him study. He may have only one rôle in the theater, but he may have a dozen in his room. A violinist will have an immense repertory before he makes even his first appearance in public. A singer's studies are never done, and I am sure that, if you inquired, you would find such artists as Melba and Caruso still working with their teachers. It should be so in the theater. It should be. Our actors fret if they have to play one rôle month after month, but that is no proof that they are ambitious. They are lazy. Why should there be all this talk of training actors, anyway? If an actor is an artist, he will train himself."

This invoked visions of a deserted Lambs' Club and the great player of to-morrow doing his present fretting before the mirror in a hall bedroom. It provoked a few doubts which I desired cleared away.

"And if he is n't an artist?"

"Ah, if he is not an artist? Well, in that case does it matter much what becomes of him?

The sooner he departs from the theater the better."

So we ceased to worry about the wretched fellow and abandoned him to his fate. The supper was over.

As we stood outside on the steps the whole city was buried in sleet. The trolley-wires crackled overhead and in a near-by avenue lighted up the sky with a fitful, blue-green glare. Mrs. Fiske affected surprise.

"What," she asked, "is Mr. Belasco doing over there?"

We were all for going over then to hiss when her attention was caught by a horse that had fallen between the shafts in the slippery street. A lumbering driver was trying to kick him to his feet. This was too much. Mr. Belasco was forgotten, and from the curb the voice of *Becky Sharp* made protest. The driver desisted, and gravely studied her from a distance. Then he spoke.

"Mind your own business—lady," he said, and at this baffling blend of manners Mrs. Fiske laughed all the way home.

II

ON IBSEN THE POPULAR

WE talked of many things, Mrs. Fiske and I, as we sat at tea on a wide veranda one afternoon last Summer. It looked out lazily across a sunlit valley, the coziest valley in New Jersey. A huge dog that lay sprawled at her feet was unspeakably bored by the proceedings. He was a recruit from the Bide-a-wee Home, this fellow, a Great Dane with just enough of other strains in his blood to remind him that (like the Danes at Mr. Wopsle's Elsinore) he had but recently come up from the people. It kept him modest, anxious to please, polite. So Zak rarely interrupted, save when, at times, he would suggestively extract his rubber ball from the pocket of her knitted jacket and thus artfully invite her to a mad game on the lawn.

We talked of many things—of Duse and St. Teresa and Eva Booth and Ibsen. When we were speaking casually and quite idly of Ibsen,

I chanced to voice the prevailing idea that, even with the least popular of his plays, she had always had, at all events, the satisfaction of a great *succès d'estime.* I could have told merely by the way her extraordinarily eloquent fan came into play at that moment that the conversation was no longer idle.

"*Succès d'estime!*" she exclaimed with fine scorn. "Stuff and nonsense! Stuff, my friend, and nonsense."

And we were off.

"I have always been *embarrassed* by the apparently general disposition to speak of our many seasons with Isben as an heroic adventure, —as a *series* of heroic adventures, just as though we had suffered all the woes of pioneers in carrying his plays to the uttermost reaches of the continent. This is a charming light to cast upon *us*, but it is quite unfair to a great genius who has given us money as well as inexhaustible inspiration. It is unfair to Ibsen. I was really quite taken aback not long ago when the editor of a Western paper wrote of the fortune we had lost in introducing the Norwegian to America. I wish I knew some way to shatter forever this monstrous idea. Save for the first season of 'A

ON IBSEN THE POPULAR

Doll's House,' many years ago, our Ibsen seasons have invariably been profitable. Now and then, it is true, the engagement of an Ibsen play in this city or that would be unprofitable, but never, since the first, have we known an unprofitable Ibsen year.

"When I listen, as I have so often had to listen, to the ill-considered comments of the unthinking and the uninformed, when I listen to airily expressed opinions based on no real knowledge of Ibsen's history in this country, no real understanding whatever, I am silent, but I like to recall a certain final matinée of 'Rosmersholm' at the huge Grand Opera House in Chicago, when the audience crowded the theater from pit to dome, when the stairways were literally packed with people standing, and when every space in the aisles was filled with chairs, for at that time chairs were allowed in the aisles. And I like to remember the quality of that great audience. It was the sort of audience one would find at a symphony concert, an audience silent and absorbed, an overwhelming rebuke to the flippant scoffers who are ignorant of the ever-increasing power of the great theater iconoclast."

MRS. FISKE

And so, quite by accident, I discovered that, just as you have only to whisper Chatterton's old heresy, "Shakespeare spells ruin," to move William Winter to the immediate composition of three impassioned articles, so you have only to question the breadth of Ibsen's appeal to bring Mrs. Fiske rallying to his defense. Then she, who has a baffling way of forgetting the theater's very existence and would always far rather talk of saints or dogs or the breathless magic of Adirondack nights, will return to the stage. So it happened that that afternoon over the tea-cups we went back over many seasons —"A Doll's House," "Hedda Gabler," "Rosmersholm" and "The Pillars of Society."

"As I say," she explained, " 'A Doll's House' in its first season was not profitable; but, then, that was my own first season as Mrs. Fiske, and it was but one of a number of plays in a financially unsuccessful repertory. And even that, I suppose, was, from the shrewdest business point of view, a sound investment in reputation. It was a *wise* thing to do. But the real disaster was predicted by every one for 'Rosmersholm.' There was the most somber and most complex tragedy of its period. No one

Mrs. Fiske as *Hedda*

ON IBSEN THE POPULAR

would go to see *that*, they said, and I am still exasperated from time to time by finding evidences of a hazy notion that it did not prosper. 'Rosmersholm' was played, and not particularly well played, either, for one hundred and ninety-nine consecutive performances at a profit of $40,000. I am never greatly interested in figures, but I had the curiosity to make sure of these. Of course that is a total of many profitable weeks and some unprofitable ones and of course it is not an overpowering reward for a half-season in the theater. In telling you that Ibsen may be profitable in a money sense, I am not so mad as to say other things may not be far more profitable. But $40,000 profit scarcely spells ruin.

"And I tell you all this because it is so discouraging to the Ibsen enthusiasts to have the baseless, the *false* idea persist that he and the box-office are at odds. Sensibly projected in the theater—"

"Instead," I suggested, "of being played by strange people at still stranger matinées—"

"Of course. Rightly projected in the theater, Ibsen always has paid and always will. And that is worth shouting from the housetops, because sensibly and rightly projected in the theater, the fine thing always does pay. Oh, I have no patience with those who descend upon a great play, produce it without understanding, and then, because disaster overtakes it, throw up their hands and say there is no public for fine art. How absurd! In New York alone there are two unversities, a college or two, and no end of schools. What more responsive public could our producers ask? But let us remember that the greater the play, the more carefully must it be directed and acted, and that for every production in the theater there is a psychologically *right* moment. Move wisely in these things, and the public will not fail."

For many false but wide-spread impressions of Ibsen we were inclined to blame somewhat the reams of nonsense that have been written and rewritten about him, the innumerable little essays on his gloom.

"And none at all on his warmth, his gaiety, his infinite humanity," said Mrs. Fiske, her eyes sparkling. "When will the real book of Ibsen criticism find its way to the shelf? How can we persuade people to turn back to the *plays* and re-read them for the color, the romance, the

ON IBSEN THE POPULAR

life there is in them? Where in all the world of modern drama, for instance, is there a comedy so buoyant, so dazzlingly joyous as 'An Enemy of the People'?"

"They say he is parochial," I ventured.

"Let them say. They said it of *Hedda*, but that poor, empty, little Norwegian neurotic has been recognized all over the world. The trouble with *Hedda* is not that she is parochial, but that she *is* poor and empty. She was fascinating to play, and I suppose that every actress goes through the phase of being especially attracted by such characters, a part of the phase when the eagerness to 'study life' takes the form of an interest in the eccentric, abnormal, distorted—the *perverted* aspects of life. As a rôle *Hedda* is a marvelous portrait; as a person she is empty. After all, the empty evil, selfish persons are not worth our time—either yours or mine—in the theater any more than in life. They do not matter. They do not count. They are enormously unimportant. On the highway of life the *Hedda Gablers* are just so much *impedimenta*."

"Do you recall," I inquired, "that that is the very word Cæsar used for 'baggage'?"

MRS. FISKE

Whereat Mrs. Fiske smiled so approvingly that I knew poor *Hedda* would be "impedimenta" to the end of the chapter.

"But she is universal," said Mrs. Fiske, suddenly remembering that some one had dared to call Ibsen parochial. "She was recognized all over the world. London saw her at every dinner-table, and I have watched a great auditorium in the far West—a place as large as our Metropolitan—held enthralled by that brilliant comedy."

"Which I myself have seen played as tragedy."

"Of course you have," she answered in triumph. "And that is precisely the trouble. When you think how shockingly Ibsen has been misinterpreted and mangled, it is scarcely surprising that there are not a dozen of his plays occupying theaters in New York at this time. It is only surprising he has lived to tell the tale. Small wonder he has been roundly abused."

And I mentioned one performance of "John Gabriel Borkmann" in which only the central figure was adequately played and which moved one of the newspaper scribes to an outburst

ON IBSEN THE POPULAR

against, not the players, but against Ibsen as the "sick man of the theater."

"Exactly," said Mrs. Fiske. "And so it has always gone. Ibsen's plays are too majestic and too complex to be so maltreated. To read 'Borkmann' in the light of some knowledge of life is to marvel at the blending of human insight and poetic feeling. How beautiful, how wonderful is that last walk with *Ella* through the mists! But played without understanding, this and the others are less than nothing at all. Yet with the published texts in every bookstore, there is no excuse for any of us blaming the outrage on Ibsen. We would attend a high-school orchestra's performance of a Wagnerian score and blame the result on Wagner. Or would we? We would have once."

And we paused to recall how curiously alike had been the advent and development of these two giants as irresistible forces.

"It was not so very long ago," said Mrs. Fiske, with great satisfaction, "that a goodly number of well-meaning people dismissed Wagner with tolerant smiles. There is a goodly number of the same sort of people who still wave Ibsen away. Extraordinary questions are still asked with regard to him. The same sort of dazing questions, I suppose, were once asked about Wagner. I myself have been asked, 'Why do you like Ibsen?' And to such a question, after the first staggering moment, one perhaps finds voice to ask in return, 'Why do you like the ocean?' Or, 'Why do you like a sunrise above the mountain peak?' Or, possibly, 'What do you find interesting in Niagara?'

"But, then, the key is given in those delightful letters after 'An Enemy of the People.' You remember Ibsen admitted there that his abhorred 'compact majority' eventually gathered and stood behind each of his drama messages; but the trouble was that by the time it did arrive he himself was away on ahead—somewhere else."

And we went back with considerable enjoyment to the days when Ibsen was a new thing outside Germany and his own Scandinavia, when his influence had not yet transformed the entire theater of the Western world, remodeling its very architecture, and reaching so far that never a pot-boiling playwright in America today but writes differently than he would have

ON IBSEN THE POPULAR

written if Ibsen—or *an* Ibsen—had not written first. Then we moved gaily on to the Manhattan Theater in the days when the Fiskes first assumed control. It seems that on that occasion, Mr. Fiske consulted one of the most distinguished writers on the American theater for suggestions as to the plays that might well be included in Mrs. Fiske's program. And the answer, after making several suggestions, wound up by expressing the hope that, at all events, they would having nothing to do with "the unspeakable Mr. Ibsen."

And so at the first night of "Hedda Gabler"—that brilliant première which Mrs. Fiske always recalls as literally an ovation for William B. Mack and Carlotta Nillson, eleventh-hour choices both—there was nothing for the aforesaid writer to do but to stand in the lobby and mutter unprintable nothings about the taste, personal appearance, and moral character of those who were misguidedly crowding to the doors. But what had he *wanted* her to play? The recollection was quite too much for Mrs. Fiske.

"You'll never believe me," she said, amid her laughter. "But he suggested *Adrienne*

MRS. FISKE

Lecouvreur, *Mrs. Haller*, and *Pauline* in 'The Lady of Lyons.'"

A good deal of water has passed under the bridge since then, but even when the Fiskes came to give "Rosmersholm" there was enough lingering heresy to make them want to give that most difficult of them all a production so perfect that none could miss its meaning or escape its spell.

"I had set my heart on it," she said sadly. "It was to have been our great work. I was bound that 'Rosmersholm' should be right if we had to go to the ends of the earth for our cast. Mr. Fiske agreed. I do not know what other manager there has been in our time from whom I could have had such whole-hearted coöperation in the quest of the fine thing. Mr. Fiske has been my artistic backbone. His theater knowledge, taste, and culture, his steadiness, have balanced my own carelessness. Without him I should have been obliterated long ago.

"Well, Mr. Fiske and I selected Fuller Mellish for *Kroll* in 'Rosmersholm.' He was perfect. For *Brendel* we wanted Tyrone Power, who, because *Brendel* appears in only two scenes, could not recognize the great im-

"Mr. Fiske has been my artistic backbone . . . without him I should have been obliterated long ago"

ON IBSEN THE POPULAR

portance of the rôle. That is a way actors have. So Mr. Arliss was *Brendel*. But we had wanted Mr. Arliss for *Mortensgård*, and of course as *Mortensgård* he would have been superb. And then there was *Rosmer*. Spiritual, noble, the great idealist, for *Rosmer* of 'Rosmersholm' we had but one choice. It must be Forbes-Robertson. I sought Forbes-Robertson. But I suspect he thought I was quite mad. I suspect he had the British notion that Ibsen should be given only on Friday afternoons in January. I dare say he could not conceive of a successful production of 'Rosmersholm' in the *commercial* theater."

"It flourished, though."

"Yes, and it was *fairly* good. But it was not perfect. It was not *right*. The company was composed of fine actors who were, however, not all properly cast. So it did not measure up to my ideal, and I was *not* satisfied. It drew, as Ibsen always draws, on the middle-class support. It packed the balconies—to a great extent, I imagine, with Germans and Scandinavians. It pleased the Ibsen enthusiasts; but, then, I am *not* an Ibsen enthusiast."

This was a little startling.

MRS. FISKE

"Or, rather, have not always been," she hastened to add "For that, you must know him thoroughly, and such knowledge comes only after an acquaintance of many years. I have not always understood him. I might as well admit," she said guiltily, "that I once wrote a preposterous article on Ibsen the pessimist, Ibsen the killjoy, an impulsive, scatter-brained article which I would read now with a certain detached wonder, feeling as you feel when you are confronted with some incredible love-letter of long ago. And just when I think it has been forgotten, buried forever in the dust of some old magazine file, some one like Mr. Huneker, whom *nothing* escapes, is sure to resurrect it and twit me good-humoredly."

That acquaintance—when did it first begin?

"Years ago," said Mrs. Fiske. "It was when I was a young girl and given to playing all manner of things all over the country. We were all imitating delightful Lotta in those days. You would never guess who sent it to me. Lawrence Barrett. Not, I think, with any idea that I should play it, for I was far too young then even for *Nora*. But here was the great, strange play every one was talking about,

ON IBSEN THE POPULAR

and it was his kindly thought, I imagine, that I should be put in touch with the new ideas. Of course it seemed very curious to me, so different from everything I had known, so utterly lacking in all we had been taught to consider important in the theater. It was not until later that I played *Nora*—emerged from my retirement to play it at a benefit at the Empire.

"No, there was no special ardor of enthusiasm then. I came to play the other parts because, really, there was nothing else. Shakspere was not for me, nor the standard repertory of the day. I *did* act *Frou Frou*, and I cannot *begin* to tell you how *dreadful* I was as *Frou Frou*. But I did *not* play *Camille*. As a matter of fact, I could not."

There had to be an explanation of this. Mrs. Fiske whispered it.

"I cannot play a love scene," she confessed. "I never could."

So it was from such alternatives that she turned to the great Ibsen rôles—rôles with such depths of feeling, such vistas of life as must inspire and exact the best from any player anywhere in the world.

"And now to play smaller pieces seems a little

MRS. FISKE

petty—like drawing toy trains along little tin tracks. No work for a grown-up. And if now I speak much of Ibsen, it is because he has been *my* inspiration, because I have found in his plays that *life-sized* work that other players tell us they have found in the plays of Shakspere."

Life-sized work. We thought of Irving fixing twenty years as a decent minimum of time in which a man of talent could be expected to "present to the public a series of characters acted almost to perfection." We spoke of Macready standing sadly in his dressing-room after his memorable last performance as the Prince of Denmark. "Good night, sweet Prince," he murmured as he laid aside the velvet mantle for good and all, and then, turning to his friend, exclaimed: "Ah, I am just beginning to realize the sweetness, the tenderness, the gentleness of this dear *Hamlet*." So we spoke of all the years of devotion Shakspere had inspired in the players of yesterday and the day before—"inexhaustible inspiration," such inspiration, Mrs. Fiske said, as awaits the thoughtful actor in the great rôles of Ibsen. She found it in *Nora* and *Lona* and *Hedda* and

ON IBSEN THE POPULAR

Rebecca West, and in other characters we have never seen her play and never *shall* see her play.

"There are," she said, "such limitless depths to be explored. Many a play is like a painted backdrop, something to be looked at from the front. An Ibsen play is like a black forest, something you can *enter,* something you can walk about in. There you can lose yourself: you can lose *yourself.* And once inside," she added tenderly, "you find such wonderful glades, such beautiful, *sunlit* places. And what makes each one at once so difficult to play and so fascinating to study is that Ibsen for the most part gives us only the last hours."

Ibsen gives us only the last hours. It was putting in a sentence the distinguishing factor, the substance of chapters of Ibsen criticism. Here was set forth in a few words the Norwegian's subtle and vastly complex harmonies that weave together a drama of the present and a drama of the past. As in certain plays of the great Greeks, as in "Œdipus Tyrannus," for instance, so in the masterpieces of the great modern, you watch the race not in an observation train, but from the vantage-point of one

MRS. FISKE

posted near the goal Your first glance into one of these forbidding households shows only a serene surface. It is the calm before the storm—what Mrs. Fiske likes to call "the *ominous* calm." Then rapidly as the play unfolds, the past overtakes these people. You meet the scheming *Hedda* on the day of her return from her wedding trip. In little more than twenty-four hours all she has ever been makes her kill herself. An ironic story of twenty years' accumulation comes to its climax in as many hours. You have arrived just in time to witness the end.

"Back of these Ibsen men and women," I put in tentatively, "there are dancing shadows on the wall that play an accompaniment to the unfolding of the play."

"A nightmare accompaniment," Mrs. Fiske assented. "Often he gives us only the last hours, and that, my friend, is why, in the study of Ibsen, I had to devise what was, for me, a new method. To learn what *Hedda was*, I had to imagine all that she had ever *been*. By the keys he provides you can unlock her past. He gives us the last hours: we must recreate all that have gone before.

ON IBSEN THE POPULAR

"It soon dawned on me that studying *Hedda* would mean more than merely memorizing the lines. I had a whole summer for the work— a summer my cousin and I spent in all the odd corners of Europe. And so, at even odder moments, in out-of-the-way places, I set my imagination to the task of recreating the life of *Hedda Gabler*. In my imagination I lived the scenes of her girlhood with her father. I toyed with the shining pistols—

"Those pistols that somehow symbolize so perfectly the dangers this little coward would merely play with," I interrupted. "How much he says in how little!"

Whereupon Mrs. Fiske shook hands with me. She *is* an enthusiast.

"I staged in my own ghost theater," she went on, "her first meeting with *Eilert Lövborg*— *Lövborg* whom *Hedda* loved, as so many women love, not with her heart, but with her nerves. I staged their first meeting and all other meetings that packed his mind and hers with imperishable memories all the rest of their days. I staged them as we sat in funny little German chapels or sailed down the Rhine. I spent the summer with *Hedda Gabler*, and when it came time to sail for home I knew her as well as I knew myself. There was nothing about her I did *not* know, nothing she could do that I could not guess, no genuine play about her—Ibsen's or another's—that would not play itself without invention. I had *lived Hedda Gabler.*"

"It must have been pleasant for Miss Stevens," I hazarded.

Mrs. Fiske laughed gaily.

"Poor Cousin Emily!" she said. "I remember how biting she was one afternoon after she had been kept waiting an hour outside a little Swiss hotel while I was locked in the parlor, pacing up and down in the midst of a stormy scene with *Lövborg.*

"And so," she went on, "if *Hedda,* and better still, if both *Hedda* and *Lövborg,* have been studied in this way, the moment in the second act when these two come face to face after all their years of separation is for each player a tremendous moment. To *Hedda* the very sight of *Lövborg* standing there on the threshold of her drawing-room brings a flood of old memories crowding close. It must not show on the surface. That is not Ibsen's way. There are

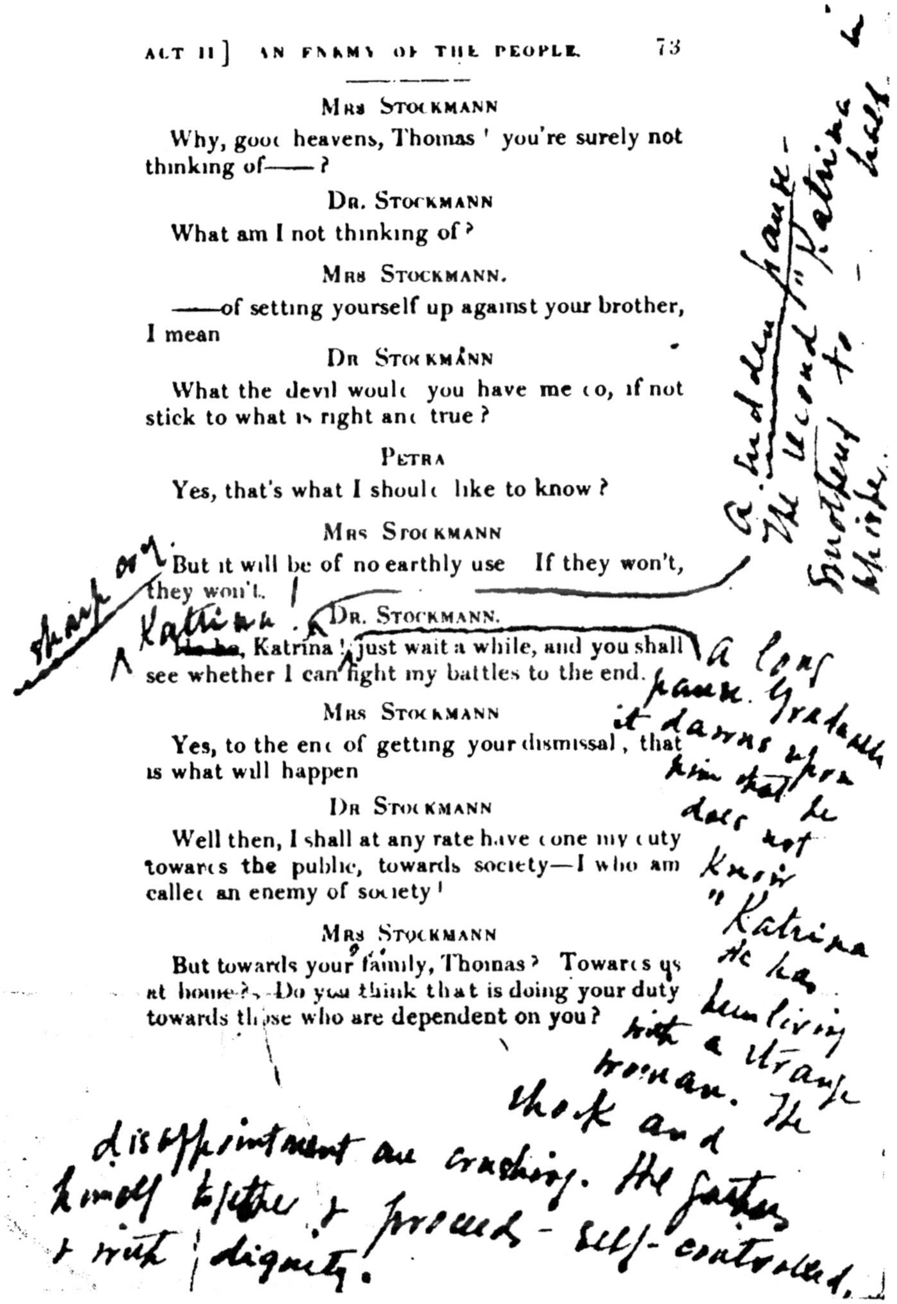

ACT II] AN ENEMY OF THE PEOPLE. 73

MRS STOCKMANN
Why, good heavens, Thomas! you're surely not thinking of——?

DR. STOCKMANN
What am I not thinking of?

MRS STOCKMANN.
——of setting yourself up against your brother, I mean

DR STOCKMANN
What the devil would you have me do, if not stick to what is right and true?

PETRA
Yes, that's what I should like to know?

MRS STOCKMANN
But it will be of no earthly use If they won't, they won't.

DR. STOCKMANN.
Ha ha, Katrina! just wait a while, and you shall see whether I can fight my battles to the end.

MRS STOCKMANN
Yes, to the end of getting your dismissal, that is what will happen

DR STOCKMANN
Well then, I shall at any rate have done my duty towards the public, towards society—I who am called an enemy of society!

MRS STOCKMANN
But towards your family, Thomas? Towards us at home?—Do you think that is doing your duty towards those who are dependent on you?

[handwritten annotations in margins, partially legible: "a sudden hush—", "The second 'Katrina' leads—", "Brothers to...", "shake arm", "Katrina", "A long pause. Gradually it dawns upon him that he does not know 'Katrina'. He has been living with a strange woman. The shock and disappointment are crushing. He pulls himself together & proceeds—self-controlled, & with dignity."]

A typical page from Mrs. Fiske's prompt copy of an Ibsen play

others—alien spirits—present, and *Hedda* is the personification of fastidious self-control. She has sacrificed everything for that. No, it may not show on the surface, but if the actress has lived through *Hedda's* past, and so realized her present, that moment is electrical. Her blood quickens, her voice deepens, her eyes shine. A curious magnetic something passes between her and *Lövborg*. And the playgoer, though he has but dimly guessed all that *Hedda* and *Lövborg* have meant to each other, is touched by that current. For him, too, the moment is electrical."

"Taking," I suggested, "its significance, its beauty, its dramatic force from all that has gone before."

"From all the untold hours," said Mrs. Fiske. "And see how wonderfully it sharpens the brilliant comedy of that scene where *Hedda* and *Lövborg* are whispering cryptically across the photograph-album while the others chatter unconsciously about them. Think how significant every tone and glance and gesture become if these two have in their mental backgrounds those old afternoons when *General Gabler* would fall asleep over his newspaper and he and

MRS. FISKE

she would be left to talk together in the old parlor.

"And I must admit," she added, with a twinkle, "that in those recreations, *Lövborg* was sometimes quite unmanageable. He would behave very badly."

"Like *Colonel Newcome*," I exclaimed.

"Not at *all* like *Colonel Newcome*. What *do* you mean?"

"Exactly like," I went on enthusiastically. "Do you remember that time when, in the days Thackeray was deep in 'The Newcomes,' his hostess at breakfast asked him cheerily if he had had a good night? A good night! 'How could I?' he answered, 'with *Colonel Newcome* making such a fool of himself?' 'But why do you let him?' This, of course, from his bewildered hostess. 'Oh! It was in him to do it. He must.'"

"Thackeray understood," Mrs. Fiske agreed. "But I wonder if he really thought the death scene—the '*Ad-sum*' scene—intrinsically beautiful."

"I suspect so," I said "It was the only part of the book he could not dictate. He had to write that alone. Anyway, Mr. Saintsbury

ON IBSEN THE POPULAR

thinks that *Lear's* is the only death scene that surpasses it in literature."

"Yet is it not so beautiful and so touching because of all that has gone before, because of all the affection for dear *Colonel Newcome* you have acquired in a thousand pages of sympathy? So it is, at least, with the great scenes in Ibsen, meaningless, valueless except in the light of what has gone before. He gives us the last hours. Behind each is a lifetime.

"And think how valuable is such a method of study in a play like 'Rosmersholm,' how impossible for one to play *Rebecca* until one has lived through the years with the dead *Beata*. *Rosmer's* wife has already passed on before the first curtain rises, but from then on, nevertheless, she plays an intense rôle. She lives in the minds of those at Rosmersholm, in the very hearts of those who play the tragedy.

"And how crucially important it is that the *Rebecca* should have thought out all her past with *Dr. West!* It is the illumination of that past which she comes upon unexpectedly in a truth let fall by the unconscious *Kroll*—a truth so significant that it shatters her ambitions, sends her great house of cards toppling about

MRS. FISKE

her ears, touches the spring of her confession, and brings the tragedy to its swift inevitable conclusion. Now, unless an actress be one of those rare artists who can put on and take off their emotions like so many bonnets, I do not see how she could make this scene *intelligible* unless she had perceived and felt its hidden meaning; nor how, having perceived and felt it, she could help playing it well. If her own response is right, the playgoer will be carried along without himself having quite understood the reason for her confession. This is curious, but it is true. I am sure of it. For, as a matter of fact, few *have* caught the half-revealed meaning of that scene between *Rebecca* and *Kroll*. It is one of the inexplicable stenches that *do* rise occasionally from Ibsen's play— like another in the otherwise beautiful 'Lady from the Sea.' It assailed me so directly that for a long time I hesitated to produce 'Rosmersholm' at all. Yet, of all the writers in America only two seemed to have been aware of it.

"But if the actress has not searched *Rebecca's* past, the key to the scene is missing. The actress must *know*, and, knowing, her performance will take care of itself. Go to the theater well

The con'ession scene from "Erstwhile Susan"

ON IBSEN THE POPULAR

versed in the *science* of acting, and knowing thoroughly the person Ibsen has created, and you need take no thought of how this is to be said or how that is to be indicated. You can *live* the play."

But with shallower pieces, with characters that come meaningless out of nowhere, could she follow this method of study?

"It would be a mountain bringing forth a mouse," she admitted; "and yet I suppose that now I always try it."

And it occurred to me that probably that delightful confession of *Erstwhile Susan's* in her present play—that harrowing return to the closed chapter back in the op'ry-house at Cedar Center when the faithless *Bert Budsaw* had deserted her at the altar—had probably crept into the comedy during Mrs. Fiske's own quest of a background for the lady elocutionist. I tried to find out, but she gave only an inscrutable smile, expended largely on Zak who was visibly depressed.

"If it is a real part in a real play," she said sternly. "That is the way to study it."

At this point Zak, who is always right in a matter of manners, rose and stared at me in

MRS. FISKE

such an expertly dismissive way that there was simply no escaping the suggestion. I started to go.

"And that," I concluded from the steps, "is the method of study you would recommend to all young players?"

"Indeed, indeed it is," said Mrs. Fiske, with great conviction. "I should urge, I should *inspire* my students to follow it if ever I had a dramatic school."

A dramatic school, Mrs. Fiske's dramatic school. But that is another story—the next, in fact.

III

TO THE ACTOR IN THE MAKING

IF Mrs. Fiske were ever to take herself so seriously as to write a book on the art to which she has somewhat begrudgingly given the greater part of her life, I am sure she would call it "The Science of Acting." Let every one else from George Henry Lewes to Henry Irving make utterance on "The Art of Acting"; hers would be on the science.

It was one glittering Sunday afternoon last autumn that I attempted to explore the psychology of that preference. We had been strolling through Greenwich Village in quest, for some mysterious and unconfided reasons of her own, of beautiful fanlights, and quite naturally we wound up at a small, inconspicuous Italian restaurant in Bleecker Street where certain wonderful dishes, from the *antipasto* to the *zabaglione*, may be had by the wise for little. Mrs. Fiske had stressed the word "science" with positive relish.

MRS. FISKE

"I like it," she confessed. "I like to remind myself that there can be, that there is, a complete technic of acting. Great acting, of course, is a thing of the spirit; in its best estate a conveyance of certain abstract spiritual qualities, with the person of the actor as medium. It is with this medium our science deals, with its slow, patient perfection as an instrument. The eternal and immeasurable accident of the theater which you call genius, that is a matter of the soul. But with every genius I have seen—Janauschek, Duse, Irving, Terry—there was always the last word in technical proficiency. The inborn, mysterious something in these players can only inspire. It cannot be imitated. No school can make a Duse. But with such genius as hers has always gone a supreme mastery of the science of acting, a precision of performance so satisfying that it continually renews our hope and belief that acting can be taught.

"The science of acting," she went on, "is no term of mine. I first heard it used by the last person in the world you would ever associate with such a thought—Ellen Terry. It may be difficult to think of her indescribable iridescence

Mrs. Fiske as *Rebecca West* in "Rosmersholm"

TO THE ACTOR IN THE MAKING

in terms of exact technic, yet the first would have gone undiscovered without the second."

Undiscovered? Who shall say, then, how many mute and inglorious Duses have passed us in the theater unobserved for want of this very science? Mrs. Fiske would not say. For her own part, she had detected none.

"As soon as I suspect a fine effect is being achieved by accident I lose interest," she confessed. "I am not interested, you see, in unskilled labor. An accident—that is it. The scientific actor is an *even* worker. Any one may achieve on some rare occasion an outburst of genuine feeling, a gesture of imperishable beauty, a ringing accent of truth; but your scientific actor knows how he did it. He can repeat it again and again and again. He can be depended on. Once he has thought out his rôle and found the means to express his thought, he can always remember the means. And just as Paderewski may play with a different fire on different nights, but always strikes the same keys, so the skilled actor can use himself as a finely keyed instrument and thereon strike what notes he will. With due allowance for the varying mood and interest, the hundredth per-

MRS. FISKE

formance is as good as the first; or, for obvious reasons, far better. Genius is the great unknown quantity. Technic supplies a constant for the problem."

And really that is all Mrs. Fiske cares about in the performances of others.

"Fluency, flexibility, technic, precision, virtuosity, science—call it what you will. Why call it anything? Watch Pavlowa dance, and there you have it. She knows her business. She has carried this mastery to such perfection that there is really no need of watching her at all. You know it will be all right. One glance at her, and you are sure. On most of our players one keeps an apprehensive eye, filled with dark suspicions and forebodings—forebodings based on sad experience. But I told Réjane once that a performance of hers would no sooner begin than I would feel perfectly free to go out of the theater and take a walk. I knew she could be trusted. It would be all *right*. There was no need to stay and watch."

"And how did she bear up under that?" I asked.

"She laughed," said Mrs. Fiske, "and was

TO THE ACTOR IN THE MAKING

proud, as of course she should have been. What greater compliment could have been paid her?"

And it is because of just this enthusiasm for the fine precision of performance that Mrs. Fiske laments the utter lack in this country of anything approaching a national conservatory. To the youngster who comes to her hat in hand for advice she may talk airily and optimistically of "some good dramatic school."

"And when he reminds me that there is none," she said, "what can I tell him? How can I deny it? I have half a mind to start one myself. Seriously, I may some day. It is an old dream of mine, for while I have never particularly admired my own acting, I have always been successful in teaching others to act.

"And how can I give him any assurance that he will encounter one of the half-dozen scattered directors likely to do him more good than harm? The young actors are pitched into the sea, poor children, and told to sink or swim. Many of them swim amazingly well. But how many potential Edwin Booths go to the bottom, unchronicled and unsung? Though I suppose," she added thoughtfully, "that a real Booth would somehow make his way. Of course he would."

But surely something could be done. In default of a real conservatory and much chance of a helpful director, what then? In order to find out, I brought from his place at a near-by table an ingratiating, but entirely hypothetical, youth, made a place for him at ours, and presented him as one who was about to go on the stage.

"Here he is," I said, "young, promising, eager to learn this science of yours. What have you to tell him? What is the first thing to be considered?"

Mrs. Fiske eyed the imaginary new-comer critically, affected, with a start, to recognize him, and then quite beamed upon him.

"Dear child," she said, "consider your voice; first, last, and always your voice. It is the beginning and the end of acting. Train that till it responds to your thought and purpose with absolute precision. Go at once, this very evening, my child, to some master of the voice, and, if need be, spend a whole year with him studying the art of speech. Learn it now, and praetise it all your days in the theater."

TO THE ACTOR IN THE MAKING

"Pantomime," I suggested, "fencing, riding—"

"All these things, to be sure," she agreed with less ardor of conviction; "everything that makes for health, everything that makes for the fine *person*. Fresh air, for instance—fresh air, though you madden to murderous fury all the stuffy people in the coach or room with you. But above all, the voice."

"Mr. Lewes hazards the theory that Shakspere could not have had a good voice," I reminded her. "Everything else that makes the great actor we know he had, and yet we never heard of him as such."

"And we would have," Mrs. Fiske approved. "It must have been the voice; it must have been. One would be tempted to say that with the voice good and perfectly trained, our young friend here might forget all the rest. It would take care of itself," she assured him. "And such a nicely calculated science it is! Just let me give you an illustration. You are to utter a cry of despair. You could do that? Are you sure it would sound perceptibly different from the cry of anguish? Do they seem alike? They are utterly different. See, this cry of despair must drop at the end, the inescapable suggestion of finality. The cry of anguish need not. They are entirely different sounds. And so it goes. Does it seem mechanical? Do these careful calculations seem belittling? They are of the *science* of acting. Only so can you master the instrument. And next your imagination."

"What," I asked, "must he do with his imagination?"

"Use it," said Mrs. Fiske, with mild surprise, while the postulant for dramatic honors eyed me scornfully. "With his voice perfectly trained, he can then go as far as his imagination. After all, an actor is exactly as big as his imagination.

"Most of us would put the imagination first in the actor's equipment. Miss Terry did, and I suppose I should. Knowledge of life, understanding, *vision*—these, of course, are his strength. By these is his stature to be measured —by these and his imagination. If I put the voice first, it is a little because that is something he can easily develop; because it is, after all, concerned with the science of acting; and because also," she added in a conspirator's stage-

TO THE ACTOR IN THE MAKING

whisper obviously not intended for the imaginary ears of our young friend, "he is likely to forget its importance, and if we put it first, he will remember it longer. The all-important thing, then," she concluded, "is the voice."

I began to chuckle.

"What," she asked, "are you laughing at?"

And I confessed to a vision of Mrs. Fiske discovering Diderot at his old trick of slipping quietly into a rear seat at the theater, covering his ears with his hands, and so, for his own greater enjoyment, transforming any performance into pantomime.

"What would you have done," I asked, "if you had come upon Diderot stopping up his ears?"

"Boxed them," said Mrs. Fiske. "The voice, then, and the imagination. And be reflective. Think. Does this seem so obvious as to be scarcely worth saying? Let me tell you, dear child, that an appalling proportion of the young players who pass our way cannot have spent one *really* reflective hour since the stage-door first closed behind them. I am sure they haven't. It would have left *some* trace. Why, the whole world may be the range of the actor's thoughts. I remember how delighted I was when I saw Duse quoted somewhere as saying that in her own art she had found most helpful and suggestive her studies in Greek architecture. That was so discerning and charming a thing to say that I'm afraid she didn't say it at all. But she should have.

"Be reflective, then, and stay away from the theater as much as you can. Stay out of the theatrical world, out of its petty interests, its inbreeding tendencies, its stifling atmosphere, its corroding influence. Once become 'theatricalized,' and you are lost, my friend; you are lost.

"There is a young actress I know, one of really brilliant promise, who is losing ground every year, and I think it is just because she is limiting her thoughts to all the infinitesimal struggles of the green-room, all the worthless gossip of the—dreadful word!—of the Rialto. Imagine a poet occupying his mind with the manners and customs of other poets, their plans, their methods, their prospects, their personal or professional affairs, their successes, their failures! Dwell in this artificial world, and you will know only the externals of acting. Never

TO THE ACTOR IN THE MAKING

once will you have a renewal of inspiration.

"The actor who lets the dust accumulate on his Ibsen, his Shakspere, and his Bible, but pores greedily over every little column of theatrical news, is a lost soul. A club arranged so that actors can gather together and talk, talk, talk about themselves might easily be dangerous to the actor in the making. Desert it. Go into the streets, into the slums, into the fashionable quarters. Go into the day courts and the night courts. Become acquainted with sorrow, with many kinds of sorrow. Learn of the wonderful heroism of the poor, of the incredible generosity of the very poor—a generosity of which the rich and the well-to-do have, for the most part, not the faintest conception. Go into the modest homes, into the out-of-the-way corners, into the open country. Go where you can find something fresh to bring back to the stage. It is as valuable as youth unspoiled, as much better than the other thing as a lovely complexion is better than anything the rouge-pot can achieve.

"There should be, there must be, a window open somewhere, a current of new air ever blowing through the theater. I remember how earnestly I wanted to play *Hedda Gabler*, as though she had just driven up to the stage-door and had swept in not from the dressing-room, but out of the frosty night on to the stage. This you cannot do if you are forever jostling in the theatrical crowd. There you lose the blush of youth, the bloom of character. If as author, producer, director, or actor you become *theatricalized*, you are lost   The chance to do the fine thing may pass your way, but it is not for you. You cannot do it. You have been spoiled. You have spoiled yourself.

"It is in the irony of things that the theater should be the most dangerous place for the actor. But, then, after all, the world is the worst possible place, the most corrupting place, for the human soul. And just as there is no escape from the world, which follows us into the very heart of the desert, so the actor cannot escape the theater. And the actor who is a dreamer need not. All of us can only strive to remain uncontaminated. In the world we must be unworldly; in the theater the actor must be untheatrical.

"Stay by yourself, dear child. When a part comes to you, establish your own ideal for it,

TO THE ACTOR IN THE MAKING

and, striving for that, let no man born of woman, let nothing under the heavens, come between it and you. Pay no attention to the other actors unless they be real actors. Like *Jenny Wren*, we know their tricks and their manners. Unless it is a bitter matter of bread and butter, pay no attention, or as little attention as possible, to the director, unless he is a real director. The chances are that he is wrong. The overwhelming chances are that he is 'theatricalized,' doing more harm than good. Do not let yourself be disturbed by his funny little ideas. Do not be corrupted, then, by the director. And above all"—and here Mrs. Fiske summoned all her powers of gesture—"above all, you must ignore the audience's very existence. Above all, *ignore* the audience."

I tried to interpret the baffled look in the no-longer scornful eyes of our hypothetical visitor.

"But can't he learn from them?" I protested in his behalf. "Can he not perfect his work just by studying their pleasure and their response?"

"If you do that," said Mrs. Fiske, "you are lost forever. Then are you doomed indeed. Audiences, my friend, are variable, now quick,

MRS. FISKE

now slow, now cold, now warm. Sometimes they are like lovely violins, a beneficent privilege. Then you may be happy, but you must not count on it. An actor who is guided by the caprices of those across the footlights is soon in chaos. A great artist, a great pianist, say, must command the audience; no actor can afford to let the audience command him. He must be able to give as true a performance before three frigid persons as before a house packed to the brim with good-will. That is his business. Otherwise he is a helpless cork tossing on the waves.

"I distrust from long and bitter experience the person in the theater who does all his work with one eye on the orchestra-circle. I could slay with pleasure the low type of stage-director who counts his curtain-calls like a gloating miser, and who is in the seventh heaven if a comic scene 'gets more laughs' to-night than it did last night. 'Getting laughs,' forsooth! How appropriately vulgar! See what an unspeakable vernacular that point of view employs! How demoralizing to the youth who comes to the theater bringing with him the priceless gift of his ideals!

Mrs. Fiske   1917

TO THE ACTOR IN THE MAKING

"After all, a piece of acting is not only a thing of science, but a work of art, something to be perfected by the actor according to the ideal that is within him—within *him*. The painter does not work with his public at his side, the author does not write with his reader peering over his shoulder. The great actor must have as complete, as splendid an isolation. The critic who is within every artist should be his only acknowledged audience.

"Besides," she added, "the audience often tells you wrong. I tremble for you if you are confirmed in your weakness by popular success. Beware of that. Perhaps you have not done your best. The audience may forgive you, the reviewers may forgive you. Both may be too lenient, too indulgent, or they may not know what your best really is. Often that is the case. But you cannot forgive yourself. You must not. It seems to me that Modjeska once told me there was nothing easier in the theater than to get applause. Remember that, and beware of an ovation. If you have had a great night, if they have laughed and applauded and called you again and again before the curtain, accept their warming kindness gratefully, but on your

MRS. FISKE

way home that night, as you value your artistic soul, bow your head, look into your heart, and ask yourself, 'Did I *really* play well to-night?' Or, better still,"—and here I caught Mrs. Fiske's eyes twinkling as if she only half meant what she was saying, but would say it for the young man's good,—"turn to the critic within you and ask, 'What was so very *wrong* with my performance to-night?'"

With which parting admonition we watched our young friend betake his thoughtful way toward the door and out into the hubbub of Bleecker Street. Then we devoted ourselves to a most extraordinary confection, the *zabaglione* aforesaid. It had arrived unbidden, as a matter of course. Even this could not banish a persistent phrase, "You must forget the audience's very existence." It lingered in the air and brought trooping in a host of old memories —old memories of Mrs. Fiske confiding her emotions to the back-drop when it was apparently no part of her intention that those out front should catch the exact content of her speech, memories of many a critic's comment on her diction and many a player's fretful complaint that sometimes he "could n't hear a word

TO THE ACTOR IN THE MAKING

she said." I could not resist singing a bit of F. P. A.'s "bit of deathless rhyme."

> "Time was, when first that voice I heard,
>   Despite my close and tense endeavor,
> When many an important word
>   Was lost and gone forever;
> Though, unlike others at the play,
> I never whispered, 'What 'd she say?'
>
> "Some words she runstogetherso;
>   Some others are distinctly stated;
> Some cometoofast and s o m e t o o s l o w
>   And some are syncopated.
> And yet no voice—I am sincere—
> Exists that I prefer to hear."

"Charming!" said Mrs. Fiske, vastly pleased. And did she defend herself? Not she. Quite the reverse.

"My friend," she confessed, "that was no part of a misguided theory of acting; it was simply slovenliness. For years I had no appreciation whatever of the importance of careful speech. Only of recent years, after some preliminary lessons given to me by Victor Maurel, have I learned to use my voice. Three hours of voice practice every day of the season —that, properly, is the actor's chore. He *must* have such practice at least one hour a day.

MRS. FISKE

With any less time than that it is absolutely impossible to keep the instrument in proper condition, absolutely impossible. Without such practice the voice will not respond instantly to every tone requirement; yet the actor must be able to play with his voice as Tetrazzini plays with hers. Indeed, he must have more than one voice. He must have at least three—three complete registers. You could write a book about this long, delicate, mysterious, and interesting science, a book that every actor should study. From it he could evolve his own method. Monsieur Maurel taught me how to teach myself. The practice followed, and still goes on. Only so, and then only in the last few years, have I even begun to speak *decently* in the theater. Before that it was monstrous, so dreadful that I should not have been allowed to act at all. I should have been wiped out. And I suspect that, if the American theater had been in a state of health, I would have been."

This confession would in all probability surprise a good many of Mrs. Fiske's critics as well as a good many of her most fervent admirers who have, I fancy, been rather flattering themselves that they were merely growing accus-

TO THE ACTOR IN THE MAKING

tomed to the articulation of a voice, "staccato, hurried, nervous, brisk, cascading, intermittent, choppy," or who had vaguely accepted an occasional moment of inaudibility as in some way an essential of that kind of acting which has inspired many a chapter headed "Restraint."

"Restraint!" said Mrs. Fiske, a little amused at its inevitable recurrence. "I seem to have heard that word before. But is it anything more than normality in acting, the warning from the critic that dwells in the inner consciousness of every artist? Is it not merely good taste controlling the tumult of emotion?

"There has been a disposition in some quarters to speak of it as a modern factor in the actor's art, but was it ever better expressed than in *Hamlet's* immortal advice to the players? I think not. Perhaps there has been more stress upon it in our generation, but that was merely because it followed immediately upon a generation somewhat given to violent hysteria in what they absurdly call emotional acting, as if there were any other kind. But that was the exception, not the rule, a passing storm, gone, I think, for good.

"It offends us all now; I think it offended

some of us always. But it was something more than an offense against taste. The actress who used to shake the very theater with her sobs, and sometimes—actually, I have seen it—knock over the lamp and tear down the curtains in the excess of her woe, was a humiliating, *degrading* spectacle. Such acting, the hysterical emotionalism of a day gone by, was ignoble, essentially *ignoble*. Human beings are far better than that, less selfish, more gallant. The woman, on the stage or off it, who wildly goes to pieces over some purely personal, and therefore petty, grief of her own is ignoble. 'My head is bloody, but unbowed'—*there* is the ideal. The quivering hand, the eyes moist, but the upper lip stiff, the brave smile—that is it. The brave smile in the face of adversity has more of the stuff of tragedy than all the outward emotionalism ever ranted, more moving to the reflective mind, touching far more readily the human heart than all the stage tears ever shed."

It was probably inevitable that the old question of stage suffering—how much does the actor really feel?—should arise then. Mrs. Fiske warned me not to trust any player's

TO THE ACTOR IN THE MAKING

analysis of his own psychology, not hers or any other's.

"I have known," I admitted, "one of our most tear-stained actresses to give forth gravely a long account of how she did it; but I doubt if she really knew."

"Probably not," Mrs. Fiske agreed. "Often we're the last who can really tell how we do what we do. I remember Réjane sitting in my dressing-room one evening and keeping us all in gales of laughter by telling of the long, solemn treatises that had been written in Paris on the significance of her way of blowing out the candle in 'A Doll's House.' She blew out half a dozen imaginary candles for us then and there, and asked us frankly what there was to that. Much to this matter-of-fact Frenchwoman's surprise, they had discovered a whole philosophy of life and a whole theory of acting in something she had happened to do unconsciously.

"It is a little that way with all of us. Does the actor feel the grief he tries to picture? It is different with different players. I should say he feels an intense sympathy. Knowledge of life and vision are his stock in trade. Why, if you have ever wept over a story or at the play you yourself know the feeling and its extent. But in his case, in addition to that sympathy, the more poignant his expression, the more cheering is the approval from the critic within him. He may be sobbing his heart out, but, such is the dual nature of the actor, at the same time he hears the inner voice saying: 'Well done to-night! Well done!' And he is glad.

"And the intense suffering he may feel in the earlier performances becomes a matter of memory. He remembers the method, the symbols, by which at first he gave it expression. He remembers the means, and relying on that memory, need not himself feel so keenly. The greater the artist, the less keenly need he feel. The actor with no science must keep lashing his own emotions to get the effect a master technician would know how to express with his thoughts at the other end of the world. I suppose Paderewski does play a little better with his mind on the composition before him, but so skilled a virtuoso can afford to spare his own feelings."

"And you?" I suggested.

Mrs Fiske as *Gilberti* in "Frou-Frou"

TO THE ACTOR IN THE MAKING

"Oh, I have found the tragic rôles wearing beyond my strength. *Hannele, Rebecca West, Tess*—such racking parts as these I shall never play again. Hereafter you will see me only in comedy. For, let me tell you something,"—and her voice dropped to a whisper,—"I have retired from the stage."

As I knew perfectly well that she was at that very time embarking lightly on something like an eighty-weeks' tour of the country, I suppose I looked incredulous.

"That's because no one ever withdrew so modestly. Usually, when an actor retires, the world knows it. I have retired, but nobody knows it. I am a little tired, and I must husband my strength. So from now on for me only 'play' in the theater. But this question of 'to feel or not to feel' which actors solemnly discuss until they are black in the face, it is all set forth here by a man who was not an actor at all."

She extracted then from under my hat on the chair beside me a little green volume which I had just been re-reading. Obviously she approved. It was George Henry Lewes's "On Actors and the Art of Acting." Indeed, it must have been some chance reference to this that started the whole conversation.

"Here we have the soundest and most discerning treatise on the subject I have ever read, the only good one in any language. Every actor would agree with it, but few could have made so searching an analysis, and fewer still could have expressed it in such telling, clarifying phrases. Some of it is so obvious as to seem scarcely worth being said, and yet many reams of silly stuff about the stage would never have been printed if the writers had had these same obvious principles as a groundwork of opinion. For all the changing fashions, what Lewes wrote forty years ago and more holds good to-day. Thus fixed are the laws of science I think," she said, "we'll have to rename it 'The Science of Acting,' and use it as a text-book for the national conservatory when the theater's ship comes in.

"And see here," she said, turning to the introduction and reading aloud with tremendous solemnity:

"A change seems coming over the state of the stage, and there are signs of a revival of the once splendid art of the actor. To effect this revival there must be

TO THE ACTOR IN THE MAKING

not only accomplished artists and an eager public; there must be a more enlightened public. The critical pit, filled with players who were familiar with fine acting and had trained judgments, has disappeared. In its place there is a mass of amusement seekers, not without a nucleus of intelligent spectators, but of this nucleus only a small minority has very accurate ideas of what constitutes good art."

"Dear man," said Mrs. Fiske as we gathered up our things to depart, "that might have been written yesterday or a hundred years ago. In fact, I imagine it was. Of course it was. I have never known a time when a writer of the stage was not either deploring the 'degradation of the drama,' as Mr. Lewes does here a little later, or else descrying on the horizon the promise of a wonderful revival. Do you know that they were uttering this same lament in accents of peculiar melancholy at a time when Fielding managed one theater, when Sheridan was writing, and when you had only to go around the corner to see Kemble or Garrick or Mrs. Siddons?"

As we strolled up through Washington Square Mrs. Fiske became a little troubled about her admonitions to the imaginary would-be actor.

MRS. FISKE

"Of course," she confided to me, "we were a little toplofty with that nice young man. For his own good we said a great deal about the need of ignoring the audience, and so forth. When he is a little older he will understand that to try to please the audience is to trifle with it, if not actually to insult it. He will instinctively turn for judgment to the far less lenient critic within himself. But I wish we had told him he must go on the stage with love in his heart—always. He must love his fellows back of the curtain. He must love even the 'my-part' actor, though he die in the attempt. He must love the people who in his subconsciousness he knows are 'out there.' He must love them all, the dull, tired business man, the wearied critic, the fashionably dressed men and women who sometimes (not often) talk too loud, and thereby betray a lack of breeding and intelligence. There are always splendid souls 'out there.' But most of all he will love the boys and girls, the men and women, who sit in the cheapest seats, in the very last row of the top gallery. They have given more than they can afford to come. In the most self-effacing spirit of fellowship they are listening to catch

TO THE ACTOR IN THE MAKING

every word, watching to miss no slightest gesture or expression. To save his life the actor cannot help feeling these nearest and dearest. He cannot help wishing to do his best for *them*. He cannot help loving them best of all."

IV

A THEATER IN SPAIN

SO nomadic is the existence of the players that any one of them who has acted for a generation in our theater has been in nearly every town and city from Boston to 'Frisco. Minnie Maddern Fiske, who made her début without a speaking part for the sufficient reason that at the time she had not yet learned to talk at all, has in her day traveled all the highways and byways of this country. Speak of audiences to her, and while you in your provincial way are thinking of New York, she is quite likely to be thinking of Kokomo or El Paso, of Calgary up in shivery Alberta, or of Bisbee, too near the Mexican border to be entirely happy in its mind. In all these art centers she has played; for that matter, she has played the somber "Rosmersholm" in all of them. Indeed, there are no nooks and corners of America she has not explored, and precious few where

A THEATER IN SPAIN

you could be quite sure of not finding her. Nevertheless, it was a little surprising when, during a cross-country tramp last summer through an abandoned portion of Connecticut, I came upon a morsel of a colonial farm-house and found Mrs. Fiske surveying me with considerable amusement from its morsel of a veranda.

Here she was, in a pocket of the Nutmeg hills, hiding from all the youngsters who want to go on the stage and from all the playwrights who feel sure her doubt as to the value of their works is all that stands between them and undying fame. Here, beyond reach of the telephone and the telegraph, she had retreated under an assumed name, an outrageously German name, although I doubt if the most ingenuous yokel would really have mistaken her for a *gnädige Frau*. The Irish and the Welsh in her, the famous red hair, and the lightning gestures—all these made prodigious fun of that umlaut she had put on for the summer. I was suffered to stay to tea, and we were soon partaking of it from an ancient table there on the veranda—a veranda dappled by the sunlight, which found its way down through the foliage

MRS. FISKE

of a somewhat raffish elm that seemed to be leaning nonchalantly on the house. We had tea and a dish of her own invention,—orange marmalade and cream,—a confection of which she is even prouder than of her production of "Salvation Nell."

It was something more than forty-five minutes from Broadway, but except for the good air and the good quiet, Mrs. Fiske was not really out of the theater. Under her hat on the chair beside her lay a published play that she had been absorbing, and pretty soon we were talking of endowed theaters. It was in the air. There were fairly audible whispers in New York that certain rich men who do for art in America what states and cities do for it abroad were rallying splendidly from the shock of the New Theater's costly collapse and betraying a certain restless desire to come forth and endow the drama once more.

"If you had five millions?" I asked curiously.

"Five millions?" Mrs. Fiske paused with her cup in air and meditated. It soon became apparent that it would take her only a few moments to spend it. "Well," she said, "I should give a million to certain humanitarian

Salvation Nell

A THEATER IN SPAIN

cults. I should turn over a million to Eva Booth to spend among the poor she understands so well. I should turn over a million to Leonore Cauker of Milwaukee, who has taken the city's pound on her own shoulders, paying for almost all of it out of her own pocket and working from six in the morning until midnight. An unusual life for a fragile, beautiful girl! Of course I could easily spend the other two million in one afternoon in helping on the effort to make women see that one of the most dreadful, shocking, disheartening sights in the world is just the sight of a woman wearing furs. The two million, I'm afraid would be a mere drop in the bucket."

"But the theater," I protested weakly.

"Not a penny."

"Ah," I persisted with guile, "but suppose you were made sole trustee of a fund of five millions to be expended in the endowment of a national theater." And then, before she had time to embezzle this unblushingly in behalf of her non-human friends, I recalled as best I could the project E. H. Sothern had sketched in the book of his memory. This was his idea:

MRS. FISKE

A national theater will continue to be a dream until it is realized on the sane and simple lines of supplying the standard classic drama, Shakesperian and others, to the poor and uneducated at a nominal price. Three million dollars would build a national theater in Washington. Endow it with an income of an hundred thousand a year, and enable it to produce a clasic répertoire for the benefit of the multitude at an admission fee of from ten to fifty cents, the object being to plant broadcast an understanding and love for the best in dramatic literature.

Mrs. Fiske's eyes twinkled mutinously.

"Broadcast?" she queried doubtfully, and then cheering up, she went on: "It might refine the House of Representatives, might n't it? But how would they dare to call it a *national* theater?"

"Because we 're not really a nation yet?" I asked, disconsolate at encountering this old difficulty so early in the afternoon, the inevitable reflection on our homogeneity.

"No, I do *not* mean that. Let 's not talk about the Civil War and California and 'East is East' and all that. In a really fine play the twain will meet. Perhaps we are not settled enough yet to have a theater *of* the nation, but we can have a theater *for* the nation. Yet how would Mr. Sothern's project meet that test? I

A THEATER IN SPAIN

suppose that most Frenchmen could get to Paris once a year or so to the Comédie Française, and certainly a theater in the Strand is within reach of all the people in little England; but neither the New Theater that was nor Mr. Sothern's dream playhouse that is to be could be called a national theater when most of the people in the nation would never see even the outside of it in all their days. The national theater must go to them. Not a resident company, but the play that moves across the country and has its day in El Paso as well as its month in New York is the natural development, the natural expression, of the American theater. Let the founders of the national theater remember that it will be their task to send not a pale carbon copy of a New York success, but an absolutely perfect achievement in dramatic art from one end of America to the other." Here Mrs. Fiske's hand was raised in prophecy. "The national theater, my friend, will not be a theater at all, but a traveling company."

We had rather good fun then in organizing it over the tea-cups and at no expense whatever. It might, she thought, give two plays a year, one classic and one new. It might, for instance, give "Cymbeline" or "The Wild Duck" and also a sparkling new comedy by some yet inglorious Sheridan unearthed in a hall bedroom in Greenwich Village. It should present its year's work, these two plays, for a brief engagement in New York, and then set forth along the road, coming to each city at the same time each year, reaching Philadelphia, say, with the first snowfall and San Francisco with the first strawberries. It would be the best the American stage could do; it would represent the highest achievement in dramatic art. It would inspire playwrights, enlarge actors, and cultivate taste. It would be a standard, *the* standard, this national theater of ours. And how much would it cost?

"Not a dollar," said Mrs. Fiske in triumph, "not a penny, nothing at all; it would *make* money."

I smiled at this, a little at the spectacle of the thwarted millionaires, a little at the evidence of the true theater woman's instinct toward endowment—one of distrust. Irving's feeling that theatrical enterprise must be carried on as a business or fail as art echoes through all contemporary commentary, the deep suspicion that

A THEATER IN SPAIN

an unprofitable theater has something radically the matter with it.

"But the most idealistic theater *can* be self-supporting, my friend. Idealistic producing is *safe*. Sensibly projected in the theater, the fine thing always does pay and always will. It is easiest to speak from our own experience. Mr. Fiske and I may be said to have had a fairly respectable career in the theater. That is to say, we have for the most part produced only plays for which we had respect. Only occasionally have we been driven for want of material to produce plays that were worthless as dramatic literature. And let me tell you this: our finest plays have always, with one exception, been the ones that made the most money. Pursuing a fairly idealistic course,—not so idealistic as it should have been,—we have had in our joint productions only one season of pecuniary loss in twenty years. There have been seasons of large profit, seasons of fair profit, and seasons of scarcely any profit at all, but only *one* season of loss. Remember that.

"I do not mean that a young producer can, with a mere wave of his ideals, establish immediately a successful national institution.

MRS. FISKE

He must have credit and he must have time. But our national theater need not be costly. The best actors? Well, the *right* ones, at all events; but I doubt if they would often, if ever, be the most expensive. Then, too, any actor worth his salt would give his eye-teeth for a place in such a company. For the training, for the prestige, for the fun of the thing, he would come for almost nothing. I am afraid few managers would tell you so; but, appealed to in the right way, the players are idealistic and responsive. Of course there are some hopeless fellows; but, then, for that matter, there are some women who would go on wearing aigrets if they saw the live birds torn to pieces before their very eyes. And there are still men who will go hunting.

"Not that an endowment could not be used," Mrs. Fiske was gradually willing to admit. "There would come in time a superb home theater, a roomy, dignified playhouse, a *theater*. In the company's long absence on tour this would be hospitable to all the best dramatic endeavor in New York. There could be a school to train pupils from all over America. There would be a workshop to which the director could summon

A THEATER IN SPAIN

the master electrician and the master decorator of the world. Then at its best the endowment would serve to reduce the price of seats within the reach of every one. It would be the happiest way, I think, if that part of it was attended to by the rich men of every city visited. Think of it, a great play perfectly presented in Denver, with the seats ranging at some performances from fifty cents, not up, but down, and with special trains bringing the people in from all the country round. It would be a joy to have a hand in such a project; it would be a privilege and an honor to appear in such a company. It would be no end of fun to play before such audiences. I'm beginning to think," she confessed gaily, "that we shall be able to use those five millions, after all."

"But what would be the permanent thing in all this? What would give the project a continuity of policy, the character of an institution? If our national theater would never stay in one place more than a month at a time, would the personnel of the company remain fixed?"

"Certainly not," said Mrs. Fiske, briskly and cheerfully dismissing several members on the spot. "Some might continue in it from one year to the next, some, perhaps, for several seasons. But the perfect company for this year's plays would, in all probability, not be the perfect company for next year's plays, and it is the *perfect* company we must have every time, above all other considerations."

"Then," I asked, "what *does* remain fixed?"

"The director," said Mrs. Fiske. "Yes, *he* is the constant in the problem. He will be the common factor in each season's work. He would pick the plays and stage them and follow them on their journey. I suppose he would have to return in the early spring to set moving the preparations for the season ahead, but his lieutenant, his alter ego, would remain with the company, his successor, perhaps. He would be the watcher, *for there must always be a watcher.* Let me tell you, it is not always the company that has been deliberately cheapened, but the company that has become mechanical and 'theatricalized,' that offends and defrauds the cities along the road. The three-hundredth performance our national theater gives in Salt Lake City must be as smooth, as finely keyed, as careful as the first performance in New York. It ought to be better. Indeed, it would be if the

Minnie Maddern Fiske

A THEATER IN SPAIN

watcher was true. Really," she said with great conviction, "you would better move out to Salt Lake City."

So if those eager to put their wealth at the service of the American theater were to come to Mrs. Fiske for advice, it would be this: "First catch your director. First catch your ideal director, endow *him*, then leave him alone."

Of course we set forth immediately to find this ideal director for them.

"I do not know who or where he is," Mrs. Fiske admitted, "but I know what he will be like: he will be an amiable and gifted tyrant."

"Wilde's 'cultured despot of the theater'?" I suggested.

"Exactly. He may or may not be a college man, but it would probably be an advantage for him to know the theater in other lands, to know what the Russians and Germans are doing without feeling that it is the beginning and end of his task to copy them. He may be a cultivated man, but he must be *of* the theater. If a man can build a bridge, we can bear up when he afterward says, 'I done it.' And our director *must* have that mysterious sixth sense, the sense of the theater, without which all is chaos, without which we often see the schemes of our dearest and best-intentioned putterers go comically to pieces.

"It is this sense that David Belasco possesses to an extraordinary degree. Whatever the extent of his vision and idealism, his understanding of the theater as an instrument, his craftsmanship, is uncanny. At one time many were disinclined to take Mr. Belasco seriously; and then in his later years he has so often confounded us with beautiful things done so beautifully that in common decency a good many supercilious words had to be eaten. Yet again and again he has devoted his rich resources to doing the lesser thing perfectly. Why he has done this, well, that is the great Belasco mystery. The exalted literatures of the theater he has avoided. I vow I do not know why. It has been through no craving for money; I am sure of that. To an extraordinary degree, by the way, almost to an hypnotic degree, as with all real directors, Mr. Belasco is equipped with a talent our ideal director must possess—the ability to teach the young to act. Even if there is no confessed school attached to our national

A THEATER IN SPAIN

theater, the director will have one in effect. That is the part of his task I used particularly to enjoy."

"And you are never abashed when they dust off and present to you that weather-beaten old saying that in the theater those who can act, act, and those who cannot, teach acting?"

"Certainly not," she replied. "In the first place, it's an imbecile saying; and, besides, I never said I could act."

And I remembered then how brilliantly they all used to play in the brave days of the Manhattan Company, how far more distinguished were the performances some of them gave then than any that they seemed able to give in other days, under other auspices. I remembered, too, how one onlooker at her apparently chaotic rehearsals had marveled at the results when Mrs. Fiske would lead a player off into the corner, sit down with him, talk to him for a while in phrases that he alone heard, but with indescribably eloquent gestures that fairly intrigued all eyes, and then send him back to the stage equipped, apparently, as he had never been before. What was her secret? What had she been telling him? I wondered audibly.

MRS. FISKE

"I have not the faintest idea. How could you expect me to remember? Very likely I was merely giving him a thorough-bass for his composition. It is often the secret of a scene, the very key to the floundering actor's problem. For lack of it you often see a performance expire before your very eyes. Recently I witnessed a play wherein, early in a scene, there was a touchingly acted, naturally moving reunion between an anxious mother and her wandering boy. She expressed the immediate tumult nicely enough, and then took it off and put it away like a bonnet. She played the rest of the scene without a trace of it Yet had she kept in mind, as the thorough-bass of her performance, the fact that whatever the text and however preoccupying and irrelevant the business, the mother would really be saying in her heart, 'My boy has come home, my boy has come home,' why, it would have colored her every word and warmed her every glance The quiet, inner jubilance would have given all her performance a tremulous overtone, the subsiding groundswell of the emotional climax. I suppose that Paderewski can play superbly, if not quite at his best, while his thoughts wander

A THEATER IN SPAIN

to the other end of the world, or possibly busy themselves with a computation of the receipts as he gazes out across the auditorium. I know a great actor, a master technician, can let his thoughts play truant from the scene; but we are not speaking of masters. We are speaking of actors in the making. Let me give you an instance. One of the several actors who have rehearsed *Barnaby Dreary* in 'Erstwhile Susan' betrayed in rehearsal a persistent, innate sunniness which promised well for the humor of the part, but which ill became the ugliness of that hard-shelled skinflint. It was in the scene where he was developing his precious scheme for marrying *Juliet*. I told him to remember always that he was marrying her for her money, that with old *Barnaby* it was a matter of greed, greed, greed from first to last. I told him to keep that abstract quality—greed—constantly in mind, and trust to it to color all his playing. He tried it, and the missing note was sounded perfectly. His thorough-bass was there. It worked. It always does.

"It is really, you see, a question of the director's searching out the mental state, the spiritual fact, of a scene. Once that is found,

MRS. FISKE

the scene will almost take care of itself. This is really the director's first task, the study of the play in its spiritual significance. It is this interpretation he must supply to his company, and there is no earthly reason why he himself should have to be an actor to be able to do it. Let him go away into the mountains, then, with the manuscript in his valise, and let him stay there until he understands its people as if he had known them all the days of their lives, until their salient characteristics and their relation one to another are fixed in his mind like the expressions of a dear friend's face, until all the *meaning* of the play is crystal clear to him. It is this meaning that he establishes at the first reading to the actors, the all-important first reading when he assembles the company before him for the first time. For the director *interprets* the play.

"Of course only a play of some depth will reward such study; but, then, that is the only kind of play our ideal director will concern himself with. Once he has mastered the play's meanings, he can breeze into the rehearsals confident that the action will suggest itself. Indeed, I am so sure of this that my own prompt-

A THEATER IN SPAIN

books are just illegible masses of—well, of mental notes, without, I am afraid, a single suggestion of practical business that might serve a stranger taking them up. You might find the word 'pensive' in the margin without any suggestion that the girl must cross to left center and gaze sadly at the coals in the fireplace." I could not resist stealing a glance then at the prompt-book on which she was working, and found the margins littered with such phrases as these concerning the various speeches: "Soften all, make gracious," or, "Sudden, passionate outthrust," or, "Brilliant contempt, independence, ardor, bravery," or, "Free, brave, individual," and I amused myself with the picture of the average New York director trying to make use of such suggestions. "As a matter of fact," Mrs. Fiske confessed, "I have always relied so largely on the help and advice of Mr. Fiske that I cannot work alone. I am colossally ignorant about the mechanics of production. Once I was left alone during a tour of the South to rehearse the company in 'The Pillars of Society.' The tangle which I finally achieved in the matter of 'business,' positions, exits, and entrances, and the like was quite too wonderful. I used to survey it from the orchestra-stalls, marveling at the ingenuity of the snarl, and wondering how Mr. Fiske could possibly unravel it in the few days given to him in New York. Of course he did succeed in relieving the congestion and setting all straight, but I remember that after the first rehearsal he was in a cold perspiration. Your ideal director should know his theater as Kreisler knows his violin, but much of the instrument I am absolutely ignorant of. I suppose fragments of the heathenish lingo have lingered in my mind. Perhaps, at a pinch, I could rush down the aisle at a rehearsal and command, 'A little more of the baby on the king!' I dare say the electrician would know what I meant, but I should n't."

Whereat Mr. Fiske chuckled reminiscently. He had just stepped out from the house with a handful of freshly written letters. He paused on the little veranda long enough to add an anecdote to the table-talk.

"I am reminded," he said, "of the only time Mrs. Fiske ever lost her temper in the theater. It was the night of the first performance of 'Salvation Nell' in New York, and we had

A THEATER IN SPAIN

come to the last act, set, if you remember, in the slums at a Cherry Hill street-crossing. There was a scene in which Mrs. Fiske and Mr. Blinn were to sit on a door-step in the deserted street, and she had asked that the only light should be a dismal ray, as from some flickering gas-jet beyond the half-open door of the tenement-house behind them."

Mrs. Fiske paused in the consumption of a wafer just long enough to interpolate:

"A very proper light for two middle-aged actors," and then went on with her confection.

"But the excitement of the first night had gone to the poor electrician's head," said Mr. Fiske. "In one mad moment he forgot everything that had been told him, and squarely on that East-Side romance he shot the whitest, brightest, most dazzling spot-light in the entire equipment of the theater. After the final curtain had fallen—that came a few moments later, fortunately—I went back to applaud everybody, and found Mrs. Fiske still inarticulate with rage. And she had been helpless, because she had not been able to order the correction she wanted. She could not even tell precisely what had happened. All she really knew about a light was whether it was too bright or too dim."

Mrs. Fiske could keep silent no longer.

"But isn't that the entire point about a light?"

And quite vanquished, Mr. Fiske retreated laughingly down the road toward the post-office with his letters in his hand. We returned to the manuscript. She had been speaking of manuscripts as completed things, whereas, of course, a new play must often be rewritten from beginning to end after it reaches the director's hands. I spoke of one distinguished producer who has a way of toiling so faithfully over a new piece that by the time the opening night arrives his name is quite likely to appear on the program as co-author. I recalled Arthur Hopkins as saying once that any director worth his salt must be fit and willing to take off his coat, roll up his sleeves, and go to work on a manuscript with the promising playwrights of his day and country. I remembered, too, that Mrs. Fiske, for all her stubborn anonymity, had gradually accumulated among the wiseacres a reputation for writing half of every play in which she appears. I hoped to find out about

A THEATER IN SPAIN

this, but only her eyes—concerning the color of which, by the way, no two chroniclers agree—made answer.

"Langdon Mitchell—" I ventured, giving voice tentatively to an old and wide-spread suspicion—a poor thing, but *not* my own—that Mrs. Fiske had done much to the manuscripts of the only two considerable successes he had had in the theater, "Becky Sharp" and "The New York Idea."

"Langdon Mitchell writes every word of his plays," she protested. "I do not recall that I ever suggested a line to him. Of course nearly every play that is finally established in the theater is the work of several minds. It must be so. I imagine it always has been so. Of the standard plays that have come down to us—Shakspere's, Sheridan's, Wilde's—we are apt to forget that what we have of them is not the manuscript the playwright first brought to the theater, but the thing as it grew in conference, altered in rehearsal, developed in performance, and finally took form in the prompt-book. Who knows what 'Macbeth' was like when the first rehearsal of it was called?

"Of course the printed classics are ready for

the stage. An Ibsen play needs no tinkering. It is not only an expression of genius and a drama technically flawless, but a tried and tested play, already purified by the fire of rehearsal and performance. And yet there's really no stopping us." Here her voice sank to a stealthy whisper, as though she suspected every little bit of shrubbery of concealing an alert little dramatic critic. "Let me tell you that once I even did a bit of rewriting on Ibsen. In producing 'Hedda Gabler' I transposed two of the speeches! And what is more, no one ever caught me.

"But with the pseudo-Ibsens and the baby Ibsens the director must sometimes labor—labor systematically as he does with the actor in the making. They are not always grateful; but what does that matter? I've never uttered all the burning thoughts I have accumulated on the vanity of one or two authors I have met, and I never will. Once, it is true, I did speak sharply to one of them. He sat contentedly through a performance of his play and then, at the end of the third act, came stormily back upon the stage. He was in a towering rage. The wonderful final speech, he complained, had been slaughtered, fairly slaughtered by the actor speaking it. 'Well, my dear sir,' I said, 'bear up. You did not write it.'"

"Ah, ha!" I observed, with the accents of a detective.

"But that happened only once," she explained hurriedly. "Really, it is false, this idea that I have collaborated extensively with the authors who have written for us. I cannot write plays. If I could, I should write them."

I must have looked utterly unconvinced, but she changed the subject.

"After all, why concern ourselves with the authors' vanity when in the theater the vanity that poisons and kills is the vanity of the actor, the egregious vanity of the 'my-part' actor. The director's first business is to guard the interest, to preserve the integrity, of the play. The actor who does not work in this same spirit should be banished. He never should have entered the theater at all. His attitude is *wrong*. From the beginning he must have approached it in quite the wrong spirit—the spirit that takes, not the spirit that gives. He should be shown the stage-door for good and all without more ado. There are really no terms in which one can discuss this bane of the theater. It simply should not be. Night and day, from the first rehearsal to the hundredth performance, the director should dedicate himself to the utter obliteration of the 'my-part' actor.

"The 'my-part' actor is the low creature who thinks of every scene in every play in terms of his own rôle. He sacrifices everything to his own precious opportunities. What makes it so hard to suppress him is the fact that he is forever being encouraged. Instead of being shot and fatally wounded by some discerning, but irritable, playgoer, as likely as not he will be rapturously applauded for his sins. The papers next day may report that his was the only performance that *'stood out.'* Stood out, indeed, as if that were necessarily a compliment! I remember that the most conspicuous and warmly applauded performance in 'Sumurun' was an outrageously protruding figure that robbed of its proper values the more shy and reticent beauties of the other playing. *It* 'stood out' like a gaudy lithograph included by mistake in a portfolio of etchings.

"It is so easy for the unthinking to mistake for distinction the 'my-part' actor's protruding

A THEATER IN SPAIN

from the ensemble. Not at the first glance do we appreciate the lovely reticence of Venice."

"Well," I offered by way of mock consolation, "Wilde was disappointed in the Atlantic Ocean."

"What a dreadful analogy! No, we need not be supercilious. We may be merely unimpressed by its pastel neutrality. I do not know what we expect; the brave colors of the Grand Cañon, possibly. So it is that we do not always appreciate at first the modest beauty of pastel playing. The lesser actor who tries hard to protrude from the ensemble is guilty of a misdemeanor; but, then, his sin is as nothing compared with the felonious self-assertion of the so-called star who not only basks in the center of the stage at any and all times, but sees to it that no one else in the company shall amount to *anything*. Thus are plays first twisted out of shape and then cast on the rubbish-heap. I remember once attending receptively the performance of one of our most popular actresses in one of her most popular plays. I was simply appalled by the quality of the company, compared with which she 'stood out' with a vengeance. Finally I saw a passage of exquisite light comedy intrusted to an actor that the manager of a fifth-rate stock-company would have blushed to have in his employ. At the end of the scene I rose from my seat, made for the open air, and never returned.

"The great people of the theater have indulged in no such degradations. Duse's leading man, Ando, was as good as she was or nearly as good. At least he was the best she could find in all Italy. The companies that came to us with Irving and Terry were artists all."

And whatever they might say of her, I thought, they could never say she was a "my-part" actor who had gathered about her such players as Mr. Mack, Mr. Arliss, Mr. Cartwright, and Mr. Mason, to mention only a few of those who shone in the constellation of the old Manhattan Company.

"Certainly," I said, "when you gave 'The Pillars of Society,' the best opportunity was Holbrook Blinn's."

"And when we gave 'Leah Kleschna,' my rôle was the fifth in importance. Do you know, the only dramatic criticism that ever enraged me was an account of 'Mary of Magdala'

Becky Sharp

A THEATER IN SPAIN

that spoke zestfully of Mr. Tyrone Power as 'carrying away the honors of the play,' quite as though it had not been known all along that Mr. Power would carry away the honors of the play, quite as if we had not realized perfectly that the rôle of *Judas* was *the* rôle of rôles, quite as though that was not the very reason why Mr. Power was invited to play it. It was too obtuse, too exasperating, yet a common enough point of view in the theater, Heaven knows. It is the point of view of the actor who tries to thrust his own rôle forward, and he should be hissed from the stage. The successful actress who seeks to have in her company any but the very best players to be had should be calmly and firmly wiped out. From morning till night, from June to September, the director must *war* against the actor's vanity."

Yet how many have treated these familiar phenomena as an essential part of the actor's nature! "If he were n't vain, he would n't be an actor at all." That is the time-honored way of putting it. "Struts and frets his hour"—why, it has always been accepted as part of the theater. Something to this effect I countered vaguely as I walked toward the run-about

MRS. FISKE

which had called for me from the livery in the village below.

"I have no patience whatever with that ancient theory," said Mrs. Fiske. "Actors have been coddled with it entirely too long. They used to say," she added with a mischievous smile—"they used to say that a real newspaper man would always be half drunk."

"*Nous avons changé tout çela*," I replied with an accent that cannot be described. The French of Stratford 'at-a-boy, perhaps.

"And we must change all this," said Mrs. Fiske, cheerfully. "What shall we do with the 'my-part' actor in our national theater? What was the procedure Mr. F——'s aunt used to recommend? Oh, yes. 'Throw 'im out of the winder.'"

V

GOING TO THE PLAY

MRS. FISKE allowed me to escort her to the play. It was one afternoon in New York when she herself was not playing, and she was fired with a desire to watch with her own eyes a fairly celebrated actor who was filling one of our theaters at the time. If he were all they said of him, she had a tremendous program of plays planned, all unbeknown to him, for his immediate future. So we talked of him as we settled back in the shadow of an upper box to wait for that expectant hush when, as Mr. Leacock says, the orchestra "boils over in a cadence and stops," when the house grows suddenly dark, the footlights spring to life, and at last the curtains part. Which was naïve of us, for this was in New York, and there is no hush; only the clatter of unblushing late arrivals mingling pleasantly with the chatter of an audience which had brought its manners from the movies.

MRS. FISKE

Mrs. Fiske was comfortable in what she fondly believed was the incognito afforded by a sheltering hat and an impenetrable veil; but had you been peering down from the last row in the gallery, I do not see how you could have failed to recognize her. One glimpse of those alert and extraordinarily characteristic shoulders, the sight, perhaps, of a familiar hand uplifted eloquently to score a point, and you would have known as well as I that *Becky Sharp* had come to see the play. But she was unaware of your scrutiny from the gallery; in fact, I doubt if there was any gallery. Her all-consuming interest at the moment was the star of the afternoon.

"Does he know his business?" she wanted to know. "He does? Has he vitality? Sometimes I wonder which is the more important. So many of these younger actors seem half asleep. Has he dignity? Most important of all, has he *distinction?* What a priceless asset for the actor or actress, distinction of manner and personality! Three of the most gifted of our younger actresses are without it. It is too bad. It is heart-breaking. Each possesses strong dramatic instinct, great intelligence,

GOING TO THE PLAY

charm, humor, emotional understanding; but each is utterly without the 'grand manner.' No matter how earnestly they aspire and work, they can never become commanding figures in the theater. That is," she added doubtfully, "unless distinction can be acquired. I wonder if it can be. Once a very clever, experienced, and splendidly trained young actress played a certain ingénue part with us. She had acting to her finger-tips, but she lacked the wonderful something her rather amateur successor possessed in a high degree. When the successor took the place, it was as if a rose had suddenly blossomed into the play. Distinction—that was it. Has our friend of this afternoon distinction?"

I refuse to commit myself. I rather thought he did have dignity, considerable of it.

"He is terribly in earnest," I confided, "and I have a sneaking suspicion it grieves him inexpressibly that his art is only for the hour, and cannot live to tell the tale when he is gone."

Her eyes began to twinkle mutinously.

"You cannot mean it," she protested. "Do actors really fret about that any more? Did they ever? I suppose they did. At least they

MRS. FISKE

said a good deal about it. I remember a delightfully melancholy bit on the subject in Cibber."

And out of her inexhaustible memory she gave me in tones of mock solemnity these stately words, set down long ago by that famous actor, critic, dramatist, and annalist of the stage, Colley Cibber:

> Pity it is that the momentary beauties flowing from an harmonious elocution cannot, like those of poetry, be their own record! That the animated graces of the player can live no longer than the instant breadth and motion that presents them; or, at best, can but imperfectly glimmer through the memory or imperfect attestation of a few surviving spectators!

"But you do not have to go as far back as Cibber," I put in. "I am sure Mr. Jefferson was feeling a little afflicted when he said there was nothing so useless as a dead actor, and I know Lawrence Barrett used to lament lugubriously that it was his fate every night of his life to carve a statue in snow."

Whereat Mrs. Fiske indulged herself in the most irreverent smile I have ever seen.

"Did Mr. Barrett really say that? Dear! dear! how seriously we take ourselves! And

GOING TO THE PLAY

how absurd when we are paid in our own lifetime so much more in money and applause and fame than we often deserve, than any mortal could deserve! But, above all, how unthinkable that any one who looks at all beyond the hour of his death could be concerned with anything less personal and momentous than the fate of his own soul, could be anything but utterly engrossed by the intense wonder and curiosity as to what his life hereafter would be! *There* is something interesting. The great adventure!

"Yet, mind you," she went on, "I am not so sure there is no immortality for the actor. Of course the prodigious Mrs. Siddons—she must have been *prodigious*—lives in the enthusiasm, the recorded enthusiasm, of the men and women who saw her at Drury Lane. But who shall say her work does not survive in still another way? The best dramatic school I know is just the privilege of watching the great performances, and I like to think that the players Sarah Siddons inspired have handed on the inspiration from generation to generation. Thus would genius be eternally rekindled, and every once in a great while, quite without warning, we seem to be witnessing the renewal of the theater. I know I felt something of that when I saw the glow of Gareth Hughes's performance in 'Moloch.' But as for carving a statue in snow—"

And here Mrs. Fiske laughed so gaily that it was impossible to be serious any more. Indeed, when she can be persuaded to talk about the theater at all, it is usually with incorrigible lightness. And as she brought her inquisitive lorgnette to bear upon the program, I felt a sudden understanding and compassion for any one who had ever tried to interview her. I knew they had tried again and again, and if the results have been meager, I realized it was not because they were rebuffed, but because they were baffled. I was sure none of the tried and trusted baits would serve. I doubted if she would rise even to that old stand-by, "Mummer Worship," the contemptuous essay in which George Moore speaks of acting as "the lowest of the arts, if it is an art at all," and one which "makes slender demands on the intelligence of the individual exercising it," the scornful paper in which he describes the modern mummer as one whose vanity has grown as

"Erstwhile Susan"

weed never grew before till it "overtops all things human." Let the interviewer ask almost any actor what he thinks of "Mummer Worship," and he will get five columns of material without the need of another question. I wondered. I investigated. What *did* Mrs. Fiske think of "Mummer Worship"?

She gazed at me with mild surprise.

"What do I think of it?" she asked. "Dear child, I wrote it."

I might have known.

"Of course," she added, "there is no end of offensive nonsense in it, and somehow Mr. Moore leaves a bad taste in the mouth when all is said and done. Many of us find it more or less difficult to keep out of the mire and pretentious, detailed exhibitions of inability to keep out of it are, to say the least unpleasant; but in the matter of acting's place among the arts, I am not sure that even our dear Mr. Lewes realized why he had been led to think so often that the actor was the less exalted and less creative artist. I suspect it was because he had seen most of them in Shakspere, an immeasurably greater artist than any actor we know of. None could be compared with him;

MRS. FISKE

yet, in the estimate of the actor's place in the arts, they all *have* been compared with Shakspere, I think. But there are times when the actor as an artist is far greater and more creative than his material, when he does something more than 'repeat a portion of a story invented by another,' as Mr. Moore has it. Yet quite as distinguished a writer has said the least gifted author of a play, the least gifted creator of a drama, is a man of higher intellectual importance than his best interpreter. Now, distinguished though he be, this writer betrays himself as one untrained in the psychology of the theater. We actors are time and again compelled to *read* values into plays—values unprovided by our authors. Think of Duse in 'Magda.' Out of her knowledge of life, out of her vision, by virtue of her incomparable art, she created depths in that character which Sudermann not only never put there, but never could have put there."

"I remember," I said, "that somewhere Arthur Symons sighed over Duse, and wept that the poets of the day left empty that perfect 'chalice for the wine of imagination.'"

"Fie upon the poets!" Mrs. Fiske agreed;

GOING TO THE PLAY

"and yet it always seemed to me that the rich wine of her own imagination kept that chalice full almost to the brim. But mind you," she whispered while we drew our chairs forward as the lights went down for the play, "as for the first part of 'Mummer Worship,' it was a little thing of my own."

When a blaze of anger from one of the women in the play brought down the curtain at the end of the first act, Mrs. Fiske devoted herself to a few moments of approving applause.

"Admirable!" she exclaimed. "That, my friend, was the essence of acting."

And I pounced on the phrase, for here was a little problem in dramatic criticism that interested me enormously, because it seemed to hold the key to half the wild confusion of thought in contemporary comment on the art of acting. "The essence of acting!" I fished from my pocket a frowzy envelop on which some time before I had scribbled sentences from two essays of the day. One of them had said, "A good actor is one who is successful in completely immersing his own personality in the rôle he is playing." And the other had said,

"The very essence of acting lies in the capacity of assumption and impersonation of a conceived character and personality different from that of the player."

I showed them to Mrs. Fiske not merely because, to me, they seemed wild, but because they seemed typically wild, not merely because these men had said them, but because many had implied them and reared thereon shaky structures of dramatic criticism. She read them with the smile with which one greets an old friend.

"Speaking as a dramatic critic," Mrs. Fiske began in a profoundly judicial manner. Then she paused, and smiled a little as though some mischievous thought were trying to dispel her judicial calm.

"But what," I persisted, "is the answer?"

"Answer? There are seven answers which occur to me offhand."

"Tell me one."

"Duse," she replied triumphantly. "And the other six are Irving, Terry, Mansfield, Jefferson, Réjane, and Sarah Bernhardt. I am sure if we went back over all the reams and reams that were written about this splendid

GOING TO THE PLAY

seven, we should find a good deal about their 'just playing themselves.' Yet when the writers on the stage brandish that phrase, when they talk of 'immersing the personality,' I suspect they are engrossed for the moment with personal appearance, mannerisms, matters of mimicry, and disguise. They are engrossed with *externals*. Yet can they possibly think these factors, incalculably important though they be, are involved in the *essence* of acting? So much of the confusion of thought can be traced, I think, to the very use of the words 'mannerisms' and 'personality' when they mean a larger thing. They mean *style*. What they see recurrent in each impersonation of a great artist is just this style. It is a part of the art of *all* artists, but only the *actor* is scolded for it. Wagner is intensely Wagnerian even in the most humorous passages of 'Die Meistersinger.' Whistler is always Whistler, and Sargent always Sargent. Dickens was always Dickens. The one time he lapsed from his own style was when he wrote 'The Tale of Two Cities,' and only those who do not love Dickens at all like that book the best. Only Charles Reade was at his best when he was not himself.

Chesterton is always extravagantly himself, even when he writes for the theater. Imagine a Barrie book that was not Barriesque, or a Barrie play that was not at all Barrie. In that sense Duse was always Duse and Irving was always Irving."

"Suppose," I ventured, "that an actor in your company were called upon to play an old Scotch gardener in a towering rage. What would be the essential thing?"

"The rage," she answered instantly, and then added in a moment of caution, "though if he did not suggest gardening and age and Scotland, the director should plot his undoing. He should want him out of the company. But the rage would be the heart of the matter, the real test of him, the essence of his acting."

"Then the essential thing is the emotion—"

"I am afraid of the word. It has been depreciated by 'emotionalism,' whatever that may mean. If it does not mean acting, it does not mean anything. No," she went on reflectively, "I have never tried before to put it into words, but it seems to me that the essence of acting is the conveyance of certain states of mind and heart, certain spiritual things, certain

GOING TO THE PLAY

abstract qualities. It is the conveyance of truth by the actor as a medium. What is truth?" And she held up her hand as if to draw it in through the tips of her fingers. "It is everywhere, in the skies, in the mountains, in the air around us, in life. The essence of acting is the conveyance of truth through the medium of the actor's mind and person. The science of acting deals with the perfecting of that medium. The great actors are the luminous ones. They are the great conductors of the stage."

She laughed a little.

"Are we getting too mystical?" she asked.

"Somewhat."

"It will do us good. But be sure of this, the essence of acting is the expression of the abstract thing, courage, fear, despair, anguish, anger, pity, piety. The great rôles are, in that sense, abstractions. So *Juliet* is youthful love, and *Lady Macbeth* is will power or ruthless ambition, as you will. Think of Duse in 'La Locandiera.' As for her mannerisms, as to the extent of her disguise, as for the difference between her rôle and her own personality, I do not remember. In many matters of externals she was careless. You know she was almost theatrical in her untheatricalism. Her make-up for *Mirandolina* and *Santuzza* was virtually the same. *Mirandolina* in that delightful comedy is the coquettish hostess of the inn. I do not remember how exactly she represented or suggested a hostess of an inn. What I do remember is that she was more than a coquettish hostess. She was more than a coquette. She achieved a sublimation. *She was coquetry.* I think of her in the book scene from 'Paolo and Francesca.' There she played the guilty lover, but she was more than a guilty lover; she was guilty love. And so," said Mrs. Fiske, "I think there must be something amiss with those definitions on the back of your envelop, for when we look on the great actors of our time, the questions those definitions raise may vanish utterly—vanish into thin air. Indeed, the greatest actors have, in a sense, always played themselves. When I remember Duse, I cannot think of her degree of success in this or that impersonation. I cannot think of her variations. I think only of the essential thing, the style, the quality, that was Duse. Just as we think of a certain style and quality

"When I remember Duse . . . I think only of the essential thing, the style, the quality, that was Duse"

GOING TO THE PLAY

at the very mention of Whistler's name. When I remember Irving and Terry, I am inclined to think that Miss Terry was the greater actor, the more luminous medium, just because, while I can think of Irving in widely varied characterizations, I can think of her only as the quality that was Ellen Terry, the indescribable iridescence of her, the brilliance that was like sunlight shimmering on the waters of a fountain. When I think of Ellen Terry in her prime, were it *Portia* or *Olivia* or *Beatrice*, I think of light, light, radiance, radiance, always moving, moving, moving, always motion."

I wish that Ellen Terry, and all the rest of the world, for that matter, could have seen and heard Mrs. Fiske as she spoke these words for remembrance.

"But," she added, smiling, "it isn't Ellen Terry this afternoon and here is our second act."

When the curtain fell again, and the house began to buzz even more vigorously than while the scene was in progress, we caught at the loose ends of our first entr'acte.

MRS. FISKE

"We made our little definition on the spur of the moment," said Mrs. Fiske, "but I think I could prove it by the great actors I have seen."

"Who was the greatest actor you ever saw?" I demanded, who have a passion for such things. "What was the greatest single performance?"

Mrs. Fiske gazed distractedly about her.

"I could not possibly tell."

"Of course not. We never can. What was the greatest short story? Shall we say 'A Lodging for the Night' to save the trouble of thinking it out? Ask any novelist to name the greatest novel, and he will say 'Tom Jones.'"

"But," said the heretic, "it might embarrass him dreadfully, poor man, if you were to ask him to name any of the characters in 'Tom Jones.'"

"Of course it's an impossible question, I know; but I should like to know what names come to your mind when you try to answer it. Suppose," I persisted—"suppose you were asked at the point of a loaded gun to name the greatest performance you ever saw, what would you say?"

Mrs. Fiske had an answer for that:

GOING TO THE PLAY

"Shoot!" So I threw away the gun and surrendered.

"But, you see," she explained, "I have had such mere snatches as a playgoer. I have been very little to the theater. Often the great actors have played here in the city when I was here, and yet, evening for evening and matinée for matinée, I, too was playing and could not see them. We of the stage who are critical, but responsive, playgoers, and who go more than half-way to meet every play, have few opportunities at your side of the footlights. So I saw Edwin Booth only when he was too old and Mansfield only when he was too young. I never saw him in his mature years. If I were to speak slightingly of him, you might wring from me the admission that I had seen him in none of his great rôles. Then I know, if you do not, how players vary in a single rôle, how unfair a chance glimpse of them on an off night may be. The worst performances I ever gave as *Becky Sharp* were both in New York. One was at the première of the play; the other was on the first night of its revival. I should not care to be judged on those. It would be absurd. They were shocking performances, both of them. Indeed, the annalist of the stage who allows himself to write positively on the work of a really great stage artist at one sitting is on unsafe ground. A really great master in any art must be studied. We may not understand him at all at first. Particularly is the critic of great acting in danger. Great actors are not so steady as great painters, composers, sculptors, or writers. They are not so dependable. I have seen Miss Terry, Duse, and others of high degree give shockingly bad performances. Personally, I am cautious as a critic. I am careful not to give an opinion on the work of an actor of great reputation until I have studied him carefully many times. I am fearful of making a blunder. No artist is so likely to be over-keyed as the really great actor, and if he is over-keyed, he gives a hopeless performance.

"There is one minor actress, however, of whom I have always been a merciless critic. That is myself. I acted 'Salvation Nell' steadily for two years, and in all that time I gave only one performance that I approved, only one that was really *good*. That solitary performance was given, by the way, in Bridge-

"Mary of Magdala"

GOING TO THE PLAY

port, Connecticut. Did you happen to be there?" she asked, with mock concern. "I was afraid not. But you see why I hesitate to play critic out of my meager experiences as a play-goer.

"Then, too, I know that some of the finest things lie unchronicled far off the beaten track. I often wonder how many of them I have not only missed, but never even heard of. I know one of the most stirring performances I ever witnessed was in a little German theater out West, and one of the most stimulating playhouses I know is the Neighborhood Playhouse far down in Grand Street. It wins one's admiration and respect at once. It is a rest and delight to enter its lobby. Rare good taste prevails everywhere, in the auditorium, in every department behind the scenes—good taste, good sense. The Neighborhood Playhouse has made no pretensions; its policy is dignified and practical. The higher and more 'advanced' dramatic literature is given careful, sympathetic, and intelligent interpretation. More than that, one is as apt as not to experience the thrill of a moment of genuine beauty here and there. And surprises are in store. The whole spirit of the thing is so fine that one cannot help hoping it will grow eventually into something bigger and of greater service.

"We must be careful, though, not to take the tone of patronizing discoverers when we tell of the out-of-the-way theaters. I remember an American professor writing home from Italy years ago of a performance he had stumbled on in an obscure and dingy theater in Venice. He was really quite impressed, and added graciously that some of our fairly good American actors might do worse than contemplate such sound and unpretentious endeavor. It was not until long afterward that he found out whom he had seen that afternoon," she said, with a delighted laugh at the recollection. "As he had not bought a program that day in Venice, it was not until she came in triumph to America that he knew he had stumbled on that out-of-the-way actress, Eleanora Duse."

"But the great names that come to mind?" I prompted at the sound of one of them.

"Well," she said, "I have played with a good many. I played with Barry Sullivan, Laura Keene, E. H. Davenport, John McCullough, Junius Brutus Booth, Mary Anderson. But

GOING TO THE PLAY

you cannot expect me to remember what I probably did not even notice at the time. And having started at three, I was such a tiny child when I played with most of those. I could not have been five when I was in Miss Keene's company. Of all those with whom I played when I was a mere baby, my most vivid memory is of J. K. Emmet, and I have never known since then a more overwhelming charm than that graceless comedian had. I played with him in New York in a piece called 'Karl and Hilda,' a momentous occasion, for it was then that Mr. Fiske first beheld me, and it was then that Emmet sang for the first time—to me sitting there on his knee—his famous lullaby. He had charm in the sense that Lotta had it, and still has it.

"So I saw a good many of the great folk in those days, but I doubt if I ever appreciated a performance as great until I saw Adelaide Neilson as *Viola*. I was thirteen then, and to this day I remember the beauty and the technic of that performance. I remember perfectly bits of 'business.' Certainly Miss Neilson comes to my mind, and moments of the great Janauschek. Then Duse as *Mirandolina*, as *Fran-*

cesca, and in 'La femme de Claude'; Irving and Terry in 'The Vicar of Wakefield' and 'The Merchant of Venice'; Jefferson as *Bob Acres* and *Rip;* and Calvé as *Carmen* and *Santuzza.* You may think of Calvé only as a great singer. I think of her as a great actress.

"But that was long ago. I do not know when in later years I have been more impressed than by the work of Frances Starr and Harriet Otis Dellenbaugh in 'Marie Odile,' and the work of Nazimova in 'War Brides.' Then do you remember the work of Miss Anglin in the lighter scenes of 'Helena Richie,' and her beautiful comedy in a one-act play called 'After the Ball'? There is a sort of *splendor* in Miss Anglin's personality, it seems to me. And certainly I must not forget the fine playing I have witnessed not from the auditorium, but from my own corner of the stage. Let me pay my respects to George Arliss in 'The New York Idea' and 'Leah Kleschna,' John Mason and Marian Lea in 'The New York Idea,' Tyrone Power in 'Mary of Magdala,' Holbrook Blinn and Gilda Varesi in 'Salvation Nell,' William B. Mack in 'Kleschna' and 'Hedda Gabler,' and Carlotta Nillson in

GOING TO THE PLAY

'Hedda.' How many of these come to mind! There was Fuller Mellish and Albert Bruning in 'Rosmersholm,' Arthur Byron in 'The High Road,' and Florine Arnold as *Ma* in 'Mrs. Bumpstead-Leigh.' There was Frederic de Belleville in 'Little Italy' and 'Divorçons'; there was Max Figman in 'Divorçons.' I can never forget the exquisite performance of Percy Standing as the jailor in 'Lady Betty Martingale.' How can I hope to tell you all I have admired! As for the best of all, I suppose it was something of Duse's. Or Terry's, perhaps. But there I go again. I do not know."

And there went the curtain again. The third and last act was on, and the few moments of reminiscence were over.

These were fleeting, haphazard reminiscences of Mrs. Fiske as a playgoer. Her reminiscences as an actress may not be set down here, for her thoughts are too much of to-day and to-morrow for the past to find much place even in her most idle conversation. We all know that the story of her life on the stage, an adventurous, multitudinous career covering nearly half a century of the American theater, would be en-

MRS. FISKE

grossing reading, but it is hard for me to imagine her ever becoming sufficiently interested in that story to set it down on paper.

After I had lured a cab out of the jam of traffic in Forty-second Street that afternoon and helped her into it, I thought, as I walked away, how amazingly long and varied that story would be. Most of the present generation of playgoers would expect to find little beyond the chapters dealing with that most significant and most productive period of her career, the years of the Manhattan Company, from her appearance as *Tess* to the presentation here and in Chicago of Hauptmann's wonderful "Hannele." But there would be many other chapters.

The story would have to account for a very small actress trotting obliviously through the children's rôles back in the early seventies in the cavernous playhouses along the lower reaches of the Mississippi. It would then have to account for the spirited and capricious Minnie Maddern journeying all over America in the hoidenish comedies of a day gone by; for the new actress named Mrs. Fiske who came back to the stage in the nineties to play some of the

GOING TO THE PLAY

most somber tragedies of our time, and to share with Mr. Fiske and the independents the mighty battle against the syndicate; then for the glittering comedienne who is even now revisiting old theaters and old friends the country over as the lady elocutionist in "Erstwhile Susan." And even then the story would not be finished.

If I had anything to say about it, which seems wildly improbable, I am sure the first chapter would tell of her appearance in "Macbeth." Every once in so often some critic, newly impressed by her capacity to represent will power incarnate, has been inspired to at least a column of which the gist is that he would like to see her play "Macbeth," ignoring the fact that she did play it once with sensational effect, although it must be admitted she was not suffered to be the bloody lady of Inverness, but was compelled to hide her light as the crowned child who rises from the caldron in the black and midnight cavern to make the prophecy about Great Birnam Wood. By way of preface, this child must exclaim:

> Be lion-mettled, proud, and take no care
> Who chafes, who frets or where conspirers are!

But, unorthodox even then, she besought him to be indifferent to "persipers." She tried this new reading at the first performance with devastating effect, particularly on the *Macbeth* of the evening, no less a person, as it happened, than Barry Sullivan. He left the stage a shattered being, but when the culprit was brought before him, he could only roar with laughter at the sight of so preposterously diminutive an actress and promise forthwith to buy her a lollypop. And he did buy it. It was probably that new and fascinating word which fastened that adventure in her memory and so brought it in time to us.

The account of her appearance in "Pinafore" would have to come later, for the juvenile companies which are described in the first chapter of so many stage biographies found Minnie Maddern already a veteran. There would have to be a chapter devoted to the time when she sang that imperishable opera for a hundred performances, if for no other reason than the rather startling one that she was not the *Josephine* or even the *Hebe*, but that lowly suitor, *Ralph Rackstraw*.

One chapter would cover the painful transi-

Mrs Fiske as *Tess*

GOING TO THE PLAY

tion period of her early teens when, at twelve or thirteen, she would step boldly forth as *Louise* in "The Two Orphans," perhaps, or as *Lucy* in "The Streets of New York," and then struggle during the next week to conceal and nullify her ambitious legs beneath the short frocks of *Little Eva*.

In that story old friends of all of us would enter for a time and disappear. Ethelbert Nevin, Eva Booth, Madame Réjane—who knows whom we might not meet? Out in Denver, for instance, we would be sure to meet Eugene Field, the Eugene Field of the needy "Tribune" days when red-haired Minnie Maddern toured the far West and tried to be just as much like Lotta as possible. Then was the Tabor Grand in its glory, that celebrated op'ry-house where Field saw "Modjesky ez Cameel" and even tried to disrupt her performance, Mrs. Fiske tells me, by a sepulchral cough of which he was inordinately proud. He would praetise it long and patiently in the open country, and then produce it at the theater in all its beauty until the ushers dragged him to the street. On little Miss Maddern, however, he would expend such flattering attention and such horny-handed appreciation that at last she was betrayed into coming happily before the curtain and blushing over a bunch of violets that hurtled down at her feet from the Field box. She bent to pick them up, and then the happiness was his, for back they were yanked across the footlights. He had tied a string to them. Not that she learned enough from that bitter experience, for after the engagement, at the farewell dinner they gave her, she was genuinely touched when Field made a glowing speech, and in behalf of the "gentlemen of the Denver press" placed in her hands a handsome jewel-case. She made a tremulous little speech of acceptance, and then opened the case. Within were ear-rings, two of them, each made of glass and each the size of a seckel pear. The fury at herself for letting them take her in still burns.

"I might have known," she groaned when I brought the story to her for verification. "I suppose all the 'gentlemen of the Denver press' in those days could not have raised ten dollars among them."

Eugene Field, wag and chivalrous comrade, passes out of the story in time, but then enters

GOING TO THE PLAY

Professor Copeland, the beloved "Copey" of Harvard, who has only to intimate that he might read a bit of Kipling at the Harvard Club to pack to the doors that New York gathering-place of his old boys. A formal and forbidding biography of Mrs. Fiske might tell of the lecture on her art she once delivered—in a moment of abstraction, I suspect—from the stage of Sanders Theater in Cambridge, but the story we are after will tell rather of the time she journeyed out there to have tea at the Hollis with Professor Copeland. The old "Advocate" boys still like to tell how they waylaid her at the station, bore her in triumph to the "Advocate" office, and so lavished their attentions on her that the afternoon was half spent before a stern messenger-boy appeared with a note for her. One glance at it, and with overwhelming gestures of despair, contrition, and farewell, she vanished from their sight. The message had fluttered unheeded to the floor. It was simply this, brief, but imperious, "Minnie, come over to Copey's."

We should meet Copeland, then, and Modjeska and Ellen Terry, and Charles Coghlan and Lotta and Janauschek. Not the Lotta of the sixties and seventies, but the Miss Crabtree who lives in sedate retirement, and whom Mrs. Fiske visits whenever she is in Boston, to come away each time filled with wonder at a charm and comic spirit that have never flagged. Not the Janauschek of the thunderous and bosom-beating times, but the kindly *Hausfrau* who used to search her memories of the palmy days as she rocked comfortably in the evenings on the veranda of Mrs. Fiske's home in New York.

And if it were left for me to write that story, I should certainly want some reference to "Fogg's Ferry," the wild Western melodrama with which in the early eighties Miss Maddern herself came out of the West. Only the other day the man who wrote it passed on. It was her first appearance in our part of the country as a star, and she could not have been more than sixteen at the time. Not from her, but as a friend of a friend of Frohman's, I learned how profound was the impression she made then on two young adventurers of the theater who crossed her trail in Boston and aspired to place her under contract forever and ever. One was named Charles Frohman, the other was named David Belasco. One evening they met in the

GOING TO THE PLAY

lobby of the old Boston Museum and poured forth to each other their faith in the new star that had shot across the theatrical firmament. Soon Frohman became so worked up that he borrowed two dollars and hurried away. It is not puzzling that he should have had to borrow that staggering sum in those lean days, but it is a little mysterious that Belasco should have had it to lend. With it Frohman made his way to a florist's and demanded as fine a bouquet as his funds would buy. Then, with his arms full of flowers and his head full of dreams, he made for the theater where "Fogg's Ferry" was the bill. As he approached the alley leading to the stage-door his heart sank at a strange apparition. There, entering the same alley, with the same token under his arm, was the young Belasco. It was too much. The two met at the stage-door, each grimly determined that his flowers and his offer should go in first. A scuffle followed, and soon the stage-hands were rushing to the heroine of the story with accounts of the pitched battle between her admirers. She could not have guessed that the fight for her favor was between two who would achieve international reputation in the theater of twenty years after. She was merely gratified, exhilarated, and delighted beyond measure by the flowers and the fight. I have never been able to learn whose bouquet did pass the door first, but I suspect it was Frohman's, for thirty years later when he hobbled back-stage at the Hudson Theater while she was playing there in "The High Road," his first greeting was, "Did you keep the flowers?" Whereat she beamed upon him and held out both her hands.

"O my dear Mr. Frohman," she said, "would that I could have!"

But then, that is just a scrap from a story I hope will be written one of these fine days—by somebody else.

VI

POSTSCRIPT

SO many actors have entered Mrs. Fiske's company and come out of it better actors, so many youngsters have gone to her for advice and come away with a widened vision and renewed inspiration, that there has long been a call for some exposition of her "theater wisdom," some expression of the philosophy of one who has always been vaguely accounted "the most interesting woman on the American stage." It would have been a hopeless task to overcome her diffidence and preoccupation sufficiently to persuade her to write her own treatise; it would have been unthinkably out of character for her to sign her name to another's screed, as many of our players do. There seemed to be no other way than for some one who knew her to summon his memories of casual and incautious conversations, to chronicle her table-talk, faintly, but faithfully. That is how the pre-

MRS. FISKE

ceding chapters came to be written. If the reader has not found them entertaining and stimulating, the fault is not Mrs. Fiske's.

Her sentiments on the repertory idea aroused the most debate. I think her position in the matter is essentially sound and salutary. She would give to each "movement" in the theater, to each person with a project, large or small, this simple and single ideal—the best possible performance of the immediate play in hand. Aim for that directly and for that alone. Then the training of the actors, the encouragement of playwrights, the upbuilding of a responsive public, and the slow formation of a national theater will take care of themselves.

The instinct that the play's the thing has given Mrs. Fiske's career its character The Fiske productions make a notable list in the history of the American stage, but I like to believe it was less the result of a self-conscious, high-minded purpose to bestow good things on the American public than of a succession of compelling and disinterested enthusiasms for the good plays as they came along. I am sure that on the several occasions when Mrs. Fiske accepted comparatively unimportant rôles in her

POSTSCRIPT

own productions, it was not in any showy mood of self-effacement, but because of her absorption in the play itself; because she really cared about nothing except the immediate objectification of a play she happened to admire. She would care a great deal about that, and not much about its effect on her personal fame and fortune. Therefore when she told me that she would guard her health by playing only light comedies for the rest of her days, I was not at all impressed. If a racking tragedy happened to intrigue her to-morrow, I think she would plunge into rehearsals before the day was done.

The most familiar answer to Mrs. Fiske's contentions as to repertory is the defense of such a theater as a place of experiments, a laboratory for plays. The most familiar example cited is the Irish Players and their "Playboy of the Western World." Where would the "Playboy" have been had it not been for the repertory idea? To which, I feel sure, Mrs. Fiske would make unabashed answer somewhat as follows:

"Where is it now? Where was it ever? What has become of it? Why did it not run for half a season in New York? After all, we are not so very *rich* in great plays. Why had it only spasmodic and more or less disorderly production? Why has not the great theater-going public of America seen it for that public's own welfare? The 'Playboy' has been lost because—is it not true?—it was so unfortunate as to have been born and caught in a 'movement'—a repertory movement; one of the finest and most idealistic, too. So 'The Playboy' has been lost to the public of this generation unless some first-rate specialist will catch it up and give it a straight-from-the-shoulder professional presentation. Of course it is shameful that a specialist did *not* do this in the first place."

The best answer, however, to Mrs. Fiske's contentions as to repertory is to be found, I think, in her own testimony as to the difficulty, the tremendous difficulty, of assembling the ideal cast, search where you may and spend what you will. It is her point that no one company, however resourceful, can be adjusted to a series of plays as satisfactorily as the separate companies a director might assemble for each separate play. Yet the finding of the ideally appropriate company is no easy task.

POSTSCRIPT

Only once in twenty years did the Fiskes accomplish it to her satisfaction. She describes, for instance, the perfect cast she contemplated for "Rosmersholm" and how it escaped her. For it is one thing to select the perfect cast, and quite another to assemble it when a hundred other inclinations and a dozen other contracts are working against the idealistic, but baffled, director. "A perfectly adequate and successful stage representation of a play," says Bernard Shaw, "requires a combination of circumstances so fortunate that I doubt whether it has ever occurred in the history of the world." That is why Mr. Shaw insists on publishing and acting (within the brackets) his own pieces, and that is why I am not at all sure a well-rounded, flexible company would not fit any play as well as the special company its producer might be able to gather together at any one time in the scramble and hubbub of the Rialto.

Furthermore, I believe that such a fixed company, continuing from season to season, is necessary in order to give a national theater continuity in the public mind. Without the magnet of some such favorite and familiar personality, I think another "Rosmersholm," though

MRS. FISKE

superbly played, would not draw the crowds to the theater. In 1907 and 1908 "Rosmersholm" did move in majestic triumph across this country; but I do not think the people went to see "Rosmersholm." I think they went to see Mrs. Fiske.

And speaking of "Rosmersholm," let me smuggle in here this letter, which touches on her great adventure with that tragedy. Mrs. Fiske writes to me:

I wish I had realized during some one of our many idle and pleasant conversations how fully your alarmingly long memory would reconstruct them for the series you have been giving forth in *The Century*. Then in a guilefully casual and studied manner I might have let fall a few of the observations I should really enjoy making, a few of the things on which I should like to free my mind.

I wish I had taken a little fling at the reckless writing that occasionally makes the way harder and more discouraging for those who want to do the good things in the theater. Let me give you a sample from a current magazine, not because it is particularly important, but because it happens to be at hand. Some one, apropos of America's inhospitality to the loftier literature of the theater, has just said I piled up heavy losses for my manager with my "tragedies of 'Hannele' and of 'Rosmersholm,' whose lovers threw themselves into the mill-race and committed mill-race-

Mrs. Fiske as *Hannele*

POSTSCRIPT

suicide." What else, he asks, could have happened where the national idol was to be Charlie Chaplin?

Now this, as you know, is downright false and it is wickedly unfair, or, rather, this sort of thing is wickedly unfair to Ibsen and Hauptmann and America and me. As a matter of fact, in half a season "Rosmersholm" made a pleasant profit of forty thousand dollars. If any one at this late date is to make casual reference to "Rosmersholm," I think it would be just as well to say the significant thing, and the significant thing about "Rosmersholm" is that in the United States alone of all countries, in this baby-land of the Western world, that most somber tragedy of our time achieved a run of nearly two hundred consecutive performances at a profit. How wonderful! Nowhere else has it happened.

As to "Hannele," it was given for only a few performances in New York and Chicago, but that was all that was ever intended. It was purely a labor of love. We never dreamed of such an absurd project as playing a long season with anything so arduous, so hazardous, and so fearfully expensive. It calls for a chorus of Heaven knows how many and for a formidable orchestra, parts of the production that could not possibly be found outside the biggest cities. "Hannele" was not satisfying, not *right*, at the Lyceum in New York, too small a theater for its essential illusions. We had no sooner tried it there than we realized that we had been wrong in declining the invitation to present it at the New Theater; and after ten days, instead of the two weeks contemplated, we resumed "The Pillars of Society," a popular success, which

MRS. FISKE

was the regular bill of the season, whereas "Hannele," of course, was just a little something on the side with which we were indulging its friends and ourselves.

Its great beauty, which was only partly revealed at the Lyceum and which, nevertheless, won great praise from high places, was completely manifest at the spacious Grand Opera House in Chicago, where we were able to secure parts of the fine Thomas orchestra for the lovely music. We gave it for three or four special matinées, and it was superb. As a matter of fact, I think it about paid for itself; but even if it did not, the distinction it gave the entire engagement—the swell of the wake of it—was of incalculable value to us at the time and long afterward, lifting us all to a higher level. Though "Hannele" never made money, and was not expected to, I think it was probably one of the wisest enterprises Mr. Fiske and I ever undertook. It had a great and measurable value, as any one could have seen who had that mysterious and delicate something which, for lack of a clearer phrase, I must call the sense of the theater.

You must have this sense inborn and carefully developed if you would do in the theater the less obvious and more difficult tasks such as "Rosmersholm" and "Hannele." Only so can you stand alone, and you *must stand alone*. You must make your own blunders, must cheerfully accept your own mistakes as part of the scheme of things. You must not allow yourself to be advised, cautioned, influenced, persuaded this way and that. If Mr. Fiske and I had listened to the kind and earnest advice of those who had our best interests at heart, we would have thrown away a won-

POSTSCRIPT

derful dramatic property—none other than "Becky Sharp." Like many another play that has thrived enormously, "Becky," in its first stages, was a gigantic failure. We were begged to withdraw it. The trouble, every one said, was with the play and with my acting. The trouble was *not* with the play. So far as I remember, not a line of it was ever changed after the opening night at the old Fifth Avenue. The trouble was with *me*. The trouble was with my individual performance, and I knew that immediately. A great curiosity, an intense and satisfying interest in Thackeray, drew crowds to the play from the first, but they dispersed gloomy, dissatisfied, ominous. By the second week the crowds were even larger, but by this time they were happy crowds. I tell you this little bit of history because it illustrates the fact that the producer must be able to detect real failure from the beginning. Except in one instance, Mr. Fiske and I have recognized our real failures immediately and made short work of them.

One beautiful thing we did throw away. This was "Lady Betty Martingale" by John Luther Long. It had great faults, but they were the kind you could remedy in two days. Properly nursed, the play would have developed the priceless quality of delicate charm, and I think I owe it to Mr. Long to shout this from the housetops. All the long faces that hover close when success does not immediately perch upon one's banner gathered about "Lady Betty Martingale." All those who could not see, who could not instantly and instinctively reach the psychological root of the trouble, closed in upon the play and a beautiful thing was crushed to death and lost to the American theater. If you have a *sense of the theater,* you can rely on that to tell you, and with that reliance wave aside the kindly disposed grave-diggers who again and again will assemble beside your dearest efforts.

Among the most disheartening and dangerous of these advisers, you will often find those closest to you, your dearest friends, members of your own family, perhaps, loving, anxious, and knowing nothing whatever about the theater. A beloved aunt implored me not to produce "Tess of the d'Urbervilles," and I was so young at the time, so far from learning the bitter lesson of making my own decisions and obeying my own instinct, that I almost yielded to her prayers. Yet "Tess" has been the sturdy foundation of all that followed, good and bad. There comes to mind as I write you a precious bit of advice I received the other day during a visit to my dressing-room by a dear friend who was all aglow with the enthusiasm of a pleasant and inspiring matinée. "Oh, why," she exclaimed, "—why do you not always play comedy!" I do not know exactly what she meant. They are difficult to follow, these people. Their mental processes, as far as the theater is concerned, are unfathomable to us *of* the theater. I might have answered that, much as I prefer to play comedy, I could not afford to play it all the time for the simple reason that our serious dramas have, with two exceptions, always yielded the greater reward in money. I might have told her this, but I said nothing, and it is better to say nothing. Keep your own counsel. Stand alone. Pay no attention to those who have not the sense of the theater.

POSTSCRIPT

You will not succeed always. That would be absurd, anyway—absurd and stagnating. But if you do not strike immediately the flame that rises to the sky, beware your nearest and dearest with their forebodings—their dire forebodings. It is perhaps the most tedious and boresome part of a stage career, probably of all careers. I have never forgotten a visit to my dressing-room of one closely related to me. We were engaged in giving birth to a play. The process was disagreeable in the extreme. It would be difficult to imagine anything more outwardly hopeless to one without the sense of the theater. In this case, however, I was quite imperturbable, because I knew it was all right. It was quite possible to go out and take a walk and think of other things. But my near one asked with a wrinkled brow: "Do you *like* this play?" I replied, "I do not like any play we produce, ever, at any time." The only possible answer, was it not? People without the sense of the theater cannot talk about it with sanity. I could not possibly talk of painting with an atom of intelligence, and yet how blithely people do talk of the theater, and with what authority!

And then the managers! For my own part, managers have been few, and my way has been so strewn with roses in that respect that I cannot speak from personal experience; but my long life in the theater has taught me this prayer: "Deliver me from the small-visioned lords of the theater who can be depressed when the audience is scanty or frigid, and who the very next night will glow and exult in the joy of a packed and enthusiastic house!" *Such managers are dangerous to a career.* They forget that the performance may be exactly the same. They are not relying on their own sense of failure and success. Probably they have none. They are not truly of the theater. Let them be gone from it! Away with them!

The great, substantial, foundation-making careers of the stage, the men and women who have kept the institution animate as an integral part of the life of the people, have been the men and women who stood *firm* at their several posts in that part of the world's domain which is called the theater. Theirs is the power and the glory for ever and ever.

I wish I had told you all this, and I wish, too, that I had paid a little tribute to the dramatic critics of America. There has ever been a sort of comradeship between us, unexpressed, but felt, over a long stretch of years. From girlhood I have taken them for what they were worth, hail fellow well met, even when we never met at all, and they have taken me in the same way. Their rebukes have never made me angry, because I have always wondered why they did not rebuke me more. They should have. Their friendly praise has been one of the sweetest, most warming things in my life in the theater. I do go on the stage unafraid of them and with love in my heart for them. And, the country over, I think most of them have a stealthy fondness for me. Indeed, they show it all the time.

Thus Mrs. Fiske.

VII

MARIE AUGUSTA DAVEY

IN this final chapter I submit the outline of a long and extraordinarily productive career and some remote material assembled for the guidance and convenience of the bold fellow who may some day undertake "The Life and Works of Minnie Maddern Fiske." It is possible that some day she herself, in the comparative leisure of the retirement she contemplates, will turn her attention to a volume of reminiscence. But I have my doubts. It would be a fascinating thing to read, but it will be hard for any publisher to persuade her that many people would be interested in a story that does not even interest her particularly. I may add in an aggrieved tone that the data here presented I have gathered without any assistance from Mrs. Fiske.

Mrs. Fiske's life in the theater may be roughly divided into four periods: her years as an "infant phenomenon"; her dashing days as a second and lesser Lotta; her reappearance as Mrs. Fiske, followed by the richly eventful seasons of the Manhattan Company; and, finally, the present period, which includes such idler comedies as "Mrs Bumpstead-Leigh" and "Erstwhile Susan," the vastly diverting characterization in which, as I write, she is just bringing her second season to a close.

Marie Augusta Davey—for so Mrs. Fiske was named on her first appearance in this world—was born in New Orleans on December 19, 1865. Her father and mother were both of the theater. They were "show-folks." Tom Davey, whose Welsh forebears contributed to the Celtic strain in Mrs. Fiske which no one can miss, was an actor and theatrical manager in the more primitive and more adventurous days of the American stage. Lizzie Maddern, musician and actress, was one of the three Maddern sisters who came here from England on their father's concert tours. Of these sisters, Mary Maddern acted with Mrs. Fiske until recently; while Emma Maddern, also an actress in many of Davey's ventures, became Mrs. Stevens, and it is her brilliant daughter, Emily

MARIE AUGUSTA DAVEY

Stevens, whose continuation of the Maddern look and voice and manner inspires to this day the frequent and probably infuriating suggestion that she imitates her distinguished cousin.

So Mrs. Fiske was a born actress in more senses than one. She came of a stage family as unmistakably as did the Barrymores, the Terrys, or, for that matter, the *Crummleses*. That would seem to be the best way to go about the business. A thoughtful study of the lives of the players must lead us all to advise stage aspirants to have for a grandmother a distinguished actress and at least one aunt and an uncle or two dedicated to the theater. It is customary to speak of Mrs. Fiske's first appearance as having taken place at Little Rock as the *Duke of York* in "Richard III," but that was probably merely her first considerable rôle. Just as Maude Adams began her career at the age of nine months when she was carried on, out in Salt Lake City, on a platter, so, in the theaters down the Mississippi, Mrs. Fiske must have had such easy rôles as could be filled by any actress who was "the type." It would be safest to say that she *wandered* on the stage, a walking lady who appeared before the footlights as soon as she could walk, and was intrusted with speaking parts as soon as she could talk.

Minnie Maddern had long since put the nursery behind her when at the age of four she made her début in New York. If you will turn to the newspapers of May 30, 1870, you will find in the advertisement of the old Théâtre Français in Fourteenth Street the notice of "A Sheep in Wolf's Clothing," with Carlotta Leclercq, and the announcement in capitals—in prophetic capitals—that that evening would introduce "LITTLE MINNIE MADDERN, HER FIRST APPEARANCE ON ANY STAGE." Of course it was nothing of the sort, but then this was a theatrical advertisement. Just as the photographs of the alert and perky Minnie Maddern of those days look preposterously like the Mrs. Fiske of to-day, so the reviews in the papers the next day suggest that something of the same style and quality manifested itself even then.

"Prodigies are not apt to be objects of pleasing contemplation to a healthy mind," *The World* observed, "but this Miss Minnie Maddern is made a prodigy by the absence of anything prodigious about her performance, and

MARIE AUGUSTA DAVEY

her acting is entirely unexceptionable." *The Times*, which began to be rapturous about Mrs. Fiske when she was four, described her as "the first infant actress we remember whose efforts do not relish of the familiar mechanism of word and manner." "Her knowledge of stage business, her general carriage and *the careful delivery of her lines throughout the play*, were remarkable for a child of her years," Laurence Hutton wrote afterwards, "and hers was one of the most satisfactory representations in the piece."

Far more glowing were the accounts which followed her next important rôle in New York when, some four years later, Minnie Maddern was cast as *Prince Arthur* in a distinguished revival of "King John" at Booth's Theater. Agnes Booth, who was the *Queen Constance* of that production, used to stand in the wings and listen to the grief-charged voice of an eight-year-old girl, so that from it she might take the key and the tone for her own scenes to come.

During this period Minnie Maddern, as she was called on all the programs from the first, played with many notables of the stage. So she sat on Jefferson's knee as *Meenie*, or, as

MRS. FISKE

Hendrick, laboriously spelled out the sinister deed of *Derrick* for the enlightenment of the befuddled *Rip*. So she basked in the radiance of Mary Anderson, and steadied herself amid the thunder of John McCullough, and dropped off to sleep to the crooning music of J. K. Emmet. Here is a fairly complete list of the parts that fell to her:

Duke of York in "Richard III."
Willie Lee in "Hunted Down."
Prince Arthur in "King John."
The crowned child in "Macbeth."
Damon's son in "Damon and Pythias."
Little Fritz in "Fritz, Our German Cousin."
Paul in "The Octoroon."
Franko in "Guy Mannering."
Sybil in "A Sheep in Wolf's Clothing."
Mary Morgan in "Ten Nights in a Barroom."
The child in "Across the Continent."
The boy in "Bosom Friends."
Alfred in "Divorce."
Lucy Fairweather in "The Streets of New York."
The gamin and *Peachblossom* in "Under the Gaslight."
Marjorie in "The Rough Diamond."
The Child in "The Little Rebel."
Adrienne in "Monsieur Alphonse."
Georgie in "Frou-frou."
Hendrick and *Meenie* in "Rip Van Winkle."

Mrs. Fiske at four, a year after her debut on the stage

MARIE AUGUSTA DAVEY

Eva in "Uncle Tom's Cabin."
Dollie in "Chicago Before the Fire."
Hilda in "Karl and Hilda."
Ralph Rackstraw in "Pinafore."
Clip in "A Messenger from Jarvis Section."
The Sun God in "The Ice Witch."
François in "Richelieu."
Louise in "The Two Orphans."
The Widow Melnotte in "The Lady of Lyons."

To say nothing of miscellaneous children and fairies in "Aladdin," "The White Fawn" and other spectacular pieces. In looking over this formidable list, you may be struck by the great variety of the parts, and it is an extraordinary thing that Minnie Maddern, who was an absurdly tiny morsel of an actress, should ever have had the opportunity to play the grown-up parts. Yet such was the economy of those makeshift days that she can remember going on as the *Widow Melnotte* when she was twelve, and taking to romances when she was thirteen and fourteen. When she was thirteen she was touring alone, an unabashed free-lance in the catch-as-catch-can, barn-storming theater of a day gone by.

It should be remembered, too, that the long run, as we know it, had not yet come into existence, and that many of the rôles she assumed were for a few weeks, a week, sometimes only for a night. For example, the Daveys might be quartered for a season in some Ohio city, where their daughter would go to the convent school just like the child across the street except for the occasions when some visiting star would need a child for some piece in his repertory. Obviously her schooling must have been fugitive and lacking that fine, serene continuity on which educators set such store; so it is quite the thing for commentators on Mrs. Fiske to roll their eyes and speak wonderingly of the qualities of mind and taste her works have borne witness to and her whole being revealed. Yet it is not apparent that the kind of childhood she knew is not quite as stimulating as the more conventional routine of learning that two and two make four and memorizing the exports, mineral resources, manners, and customs of Bolivia. Certainly those who enter the theater early are likely in maturity to be the least stagy. To them it has never been a glamorous adventure. To them it is as natural as life itself, as much a matter of course as the air we all breathe, as little subject for corrupting thought as the blue sky we all take for granted. And they are the aristocrats of the theater.

With the production of "Fogg's Ferry" at Abbey's Park Theater on May 15, 1882, we enter upon the second period of Mrs. Fiske's career, when she put away childish rôles and went in for rough comedy and romances. It was her début as a star in New York, and she was just sixteen. Turn once more to the yellowing newspapers, and in the New York journals of that date you will see an advertisement such as this:

FIRST APPEARANCE OF THE CHARMING YOUNG COMEDIENNE

MISS MINNIE MADDERN

as Chip in

"FOGG'S FERRY"

Charles E. Callahan's romantic comedy-drama of human love and passion.
Illustrated by a strong company with picturesque scenery and magnificent effects.

The next reviews were full of nice things about the new star, but the play received short

MRS. FISKE

shrift. It is amusing to think that the great actress of Ibsen rôles and the unequaled exponent of such high comedy as "Becky Sharp" and "The New York Idea" should have had to start forth under the handicap of having the *Evening Post* laud her "winning, childlike, innocent manner" and commend her for being "frolicsome and vivacious without being vulgar." It is only with a struggle that you can realize it was of our Mrs. Fiske *The Sun* was speaking when it gave this account of the première of "Fogg's Ferry":

There has been a good deal of indiscreet and reckless writing put forth about Minnie Maddern and her dramatic gifts, but she triumphed bravely last evening over pamphlets, paragraphs, bouquets, and friends, and won the genuine good will of her audience. She came forward like a new Lotta, young, slender, sprightly, quite pretty, arch of manner, rash in the matter of her stockings, as Lotta always was, and possessed of undeniable red hair. She had not been on the stage a minute before she had jumped under most perilous conditions to a seat on the edge of a table and established with the audience relations of the most agreeable intimacy. Her self-possession is complete. She can sing even worse than Lotta can; but she has a native gift and disposition to her calling that will not be denied expression and which, if afforded any occa-

Minnie Maddern at sixteen

MARIE AUGUSTA DAVEY

sion of growth and development, cannot fail to make her a thoroughly popular artist in her line of small comedy. She made a better impression than has been made by any débutante in years, in spite of unusual difficulties that she had to encounter.

Indeed, the contrast between this beginning and what followed in later years is so diverting that there must be room found here for some account of "Fogg's Ferry." You can obtain a faint impression of its quality from this résumé, which appeared in *The Herald:*

It opens delightfully with a view of Western domestic felicity in the picture of the home of Fogg, the ferryman, in which most of the family are drunk or gradually getting drunk on the private stock of a visitor to the family, Bruce Rawdon, the villain of the piece, who has come to court Chip, the ferryman's daughter. It may be incidentally remarked that the ferry business must be exceedingly unremunerative in that part of the country for in a landscape stretching off apparently hundreds of miles, the artist has not provided a sign of the presence of man, woman, child or beast or a place of habitation on mountain or in valley. Gerald White, the goody-goody man of the play, also turns up in the vast wilderness with matrimonial intentions toward Chip, who is dressed so as to appear to be about ten or twelve years old. The sense of propriety in the audience is satisfied, however, by Chip stating that she is sixteen years old, although she

MRS. FISKE

wears her dresses cut to her knee. The two men have at each other and Chip prevents a murder, and then, after mild courtship on the part of all three, Chip announces that she has curious dreams, not traceable to indigestion, which give her an idea she was as an infant changed in her cradle. She "feels she is a lady" and asks the gentlemen if they don't feel she is right? There being no opposition, the question is declared carried unanimously and the curtain goes down. In act second Chip is found at Judge Somebody's house, where she is governess or maid or something else unexplained. The two men are there also, still matrimonially inclined, but one of them is wooing Blanche, the proud and haughty daughter of the Judge. Here it is clear to the audience that Blanche was the other baby with whom Chip was mixed up: but none but the audience know it. Some private papers in the Judge's safe are sought by the villain of the piece, who wants to get them and then marry Blanche, and Chip is accused of the theft and dismissed the house. In act third the two men turn up, again still matrimonially inclined, and the villain proposes to get more of the Judge's papers by blowing up a steamer about to pass, and on which the Judge is traveling with a load of bonds and wills and other family valuables. Chip overhears it all and saves the steamer by firing a pocket pistol into the waters and exploding a dynamite mine securely hidden on the bed of the river by piercing the iron cylinder with the ball. After this impossible exploit, the play very properly begins its natural dissolution. In act four we find Chip in the Judge's home in an elaborate costume of embroidered satin and

MARIE AUGUSTA DAVEY

silk cut in the latest Paris fashion; we find her the acknowledged daughter, while the proud and haughty Blanche is dismissed the house; Chip marries the man of her choice and villainy generally being punished and virtue rewarded, the curtain falls. Then everybody got up and said it was a very much involved and poor play but that Miss Maddern was quite good. And they were right.

I have expanded thus on the sparsely chronicled periods of Mrs. Fiske's career not from any notion that what she airily dismisses as her "pre-historic" days were comparatively important, but for two other reasons. The detail of her seasons as Minnie Maddern is less accessible, less familiar to the present generation of theatergoers. Then, too, I think it is interesting, suggestive, and heartening that "Fogg's Ferry" should have prepared for "Rosmersholm," that out of such rough-and-ready beginnings her quality both as an artist and as a commander of dramatic endeavor should have emerged in gradual beauty and significance until she should one day stand as the loftiest artist on the American stage.

Even when "Fogg's Ferry" came to town some one on *The Tribune*, William Winter presumably, hailed her while scarcely more than a child, "as one of the brightest and most interesting girls that have appeared upon the stage," but the more truly prophetic appreciation of the Mrs. Fiske of yesterday and to-day began to come a few seasons later with her appearance in "In Spite of All," an adaptation Steele Mackaye made from the "Andrea" of Sardou *fils* and presented at his Lyceum in 1885. I remember Mrs. Fiske's once laughing gaily at her own youthful recklessness in connection with "In Spite of All."

"I think the limit was reached," she said, "when I had the impudence to stroll out and engage a company comprising Eben Plympton, John Lane (then prominent), Richard Mansfield (who had already had his triumph in 'The Parisian Romance'), and Selina Dolaro (very celebrated at that time). They all 'supported' me at the old Lyceum, and they were superb. I was perfectly dreadful, really. Mr. Mansfield and I got on very well, although my carelessness in dress annoyed him very much and he frequently remonstrated with me in the kindliest way."

Yet it was after "In Spite of All" that *The Times* hailed Miss Maddern as probably "the

An early folder

MARIE AUGUSTA DAVEY

most interesting young actress on the American stage. She has many artistic faults, but, on the other hand, she has keen intelligence, a style, so far as it has been formulated, wholly her own, unlike that of any other player and entirely free from conventionality, and a most charming personality, which attracts the sympathy and admiration of all classes of playgoers."

"Without the endowment of beauty, ungifted by the stage presence demanded by the populace, lacking breadth of figure and force of personality, she nevertheless manages," *The World* observed, "by the rarest of all gifts to seize, by some inexplicable faculty of her own, upon the sensibility of her auditors and to do the most marvelously subtle, tender and pensive bits of acting which it has ever been our good fortune to witness."

About this time must have begun that community of enthusiasm which has grown with the passing years, but which never has embraced and never could embrace all the theatergoers of America. It could never have been said of her, as it has been said of one of her sister stars, that she was "the most valuable theatrical property in America." You might as soon expect Whistler, Debussy, and Meredith to be generally popular as to expect a general acceptance of the idiom of Minnie Maddern Fiske.

A comparison with such distinctive artists is inevitable. She is wont, in her own casual analogies between the art of the actor and other arts, to make free use of Paderewski, and I think most of her admirers would see a kinship between them. Certainly when they first glimpsed the splendors of her art in her later years they must have felt something as the Gilders did when they first heard the great pianist. Richard Watson Gilder wrote to his wife:

> Paderewski! Well, you have a treat in store! He is quite by himself—reminding me of no one but the young Swinburne! His genius is altogether individual, and if the individuality appeals, fascinating. It appealed to me immensely. He is not sublime, but most intensely poetic; his touch is delicacy itself in the tender parts—fairy-like; almost sharp, certainly charmingly crisp and at times, powerful; there is a quiet alertness, like some queer new animal, sure of his prey. The hit of his playing was that minuet of his that Aus der Ohe plays. He played it very differently

MARIE AUGUSTA DAVEY

—in a way to excite you more, with his quick, strange touch and tempo, though she plays it exquisitely.

Indeed, the analogy satisfies me so enormously that I must clip still another paragraph from a letter from Mrs. Gilder to Mary Hallock Foote. She wrote:

Paderewski is one of the most extraordinary experiences in our lives. He is not at all like Rubenstein, who is like an ocean, and one of the greatest of the great, but in his way as intense an individuality. He is a little like Modjeska, so noble, persuasive, delicate, firm; and the most artistic creature imaginable, all nerves and sinew, but the body subordinate to the spirit—always. A wonderful intelligence which some artists, actors and especially musicians (above all virtuosi) lack.

In her days as a star, Minnie Maddern played these rôles:

Juanita in "Juanita," by Charles Callahan.
Chip in "Fogg's Ferry," by Charles Callahan.
The leading rôle in "The Puritan Maid," by Ver Planck and Devereaux.
The leading rôle in "The Storm Child."
The leading rôle in "The Child Wife."
The leading rôle in "The Professional Beauty" by Ver Planck and Devereux.
The leading rôle in "Lady Jemima."
Mila in "Mila, Queen of the Natchez."

MRS. FISKE

Mercy Baxter in "Caprice," by Howard P. Taylor.
Alice Glendinning in "In Spite of All," adapted by Steel Mackaye from Sardou's "Andrea."
Mrs. Coney in "Featherbrain."

In 1890 she was married to Harrison Grey Fiske,—it was her second marriage,—and, as Mrs. Fiske, she retired from the stage. As Mrs. Fiske she came back four years later. When she returned, it was as an actress of new power and new quality, a director of new ambition and distinction. The line of cleavage between the two careers is marked by more than the four years of rest and study, indicated by more than the mere change of name, although, in dropping the somewhat jaunty "Minnie Maddern" for the more imposing "Mrs. Fiske," she did add to her achievements the almost unparalleled one of making two separate reputations under different names. A list of her performances as Mrs. Fiske recalls some of the finest work our stage has known and for the most part this list of the discerning, ambitious, high-minded, painstaking, trail-blazing productions made by the Fiskes constitutes a record that has seldom been approached in the American theater. Here it is:

Minnie Maddern shortly before her retirement from the stage

MARIE AUGUSTA DAVEY

Hester Crewe in "Hester Crewe," by Harrison Grey Fiske, 1893.

Marie Deloche in "The Queen of Liars," adapted from the French by Harrison Grey Fiske, 1895.

Nora in "A Doll's House," by Henrik Ibsen, 1895.

Toinette in "A Light from St. Agnes," one-act play by Mrs. Fiske, 1895.

Cesarine in "La Femme de Claude," by Dumas, fils, 1896.

Cyprienne in "Divorçons," as adapted by Harrison Grey Fiske, 1896.

Madeleine in "Love Finds the Way," adaptation by Marguerite Merrington, 1896.

Adelaide in "Not Guilty," one-act play by Mrs. Fiske, 1896.

The Little Marquis in "The White Pink," adapted from the French by Harrison Grey Fiske, 1896.

Tess in "Tess of the d'Urbervilles," a dramatization by Lorrimer Stoddard, 1897.

Giulia in "Little Italy," one-act play by Horace B. Fry, 1898.

Saucers in "A Bit of Old Chelsea," one-act play by Mrs. Oscar Berringer, 1898.

Magda in "Magda," by Hermann Sudermann, 1899.

Gilberte in "Frou-frou," adapted by Harrison Grey Fiske, 1899.

Becky in "Becky Sharp," a dramatization by Langdon Mitchell, 1899.

Miranda in "Miranda of the Balcony," a dramatization by Anne Crawford Flexner, 1901.

Mrs. Hatch in "The Unwelcome Mrs. Hatch," by Mrs. Burton Harrison, 1901.

MRS. FISKE

Mary in "Mary of Magdala," William Winter's English version of Heyse's play, 1902.

Hedda in "Hedda Gabler," by Henrik Ibsen, 1903.

Leah in "Leah Kleschna," by C. M. S. McClellan, 1904.

Cynthia Karslake in "The New York Idea," by Langdon Mitchell, 1906.

Dolce in "Dolce," by John Luther Long, 1906.

Rebecca West in "Rosmersholm," by Henrik Ibsen, 1907.

Nell Sanders in "Salvation Nell," by Edward Sheldon, 1908.

Lona Hessel in "Pillars of Society," by Henrik Ibsen, 1910.

Hannele in "Hannele," by Gerhart Hauptmann, 1910.

Della Bumpstead-Leigh in "Mrs. Bumpstead-Leigh," by Harry James Smith, 1911.

Agnes Bromley in "The New Marriage," by Langdon Mitchell, 1911.

Julia France in "Julia France," by Gertrude Atherton, 1912.

Lady Patricia Cosway in "Lady Patricia," by Rudolph Besier, 1912.

Mary Page in "The High Road," by Edward Sheldon, 1912.

Lady Betty in "Lady Betty Martingale: or the Adventures of a Lively Hussy," by John Luther Long, 1914.

Juliet Miller in "Erstwhile Susan," by Marian de Forest, 1916.

MARIE AUGUSTA DAVEY

These plays and her performance in them are part of the richest experiences of the present generation of theater-goers in this country. Their selection for the most part, and her playing in them always, might be studied and interpreted as a continuous quest for truth. Emerging in the first maturity of her powers at the first flowering of the modern drama, Mrs. Fiske instinctively and surely identified herself with the best that was awaking in the theater of Europe and America. With the production of "Tess" she came into her own. Her *Tess* with its tragic, fateful power; her *Becky*, with its resourceful and gleaming comedy; her pathetic and ennobling *Nell*, are among the unforgetable things alongside Ada Rehan's *Katharine* and the *Hamlet* of Forbes-Robertson.

This chapter does not pretend to rehearse their manifold excellence or to elaborate any appreciation of her qualities as an actress. But this is the last chapter, and I can close no book on Mrs. Fiske without speaking of those electrifying moments of hers, those thrilling, motionless silences which, though her wonderful voice has ever been a delight to me, have surpassed in beauty and inspiration all my experiences in the theater. I can see her now as poor bedraggled *Nell,* sitting on the floor of the dismal saloon in Cherry Hill, holding her besotted lover's head in her lap, an unforgetable vision of dumb grief that transfixed us all. "Ah, to be able to do nothing like that!" Mary Garden exclaimed, and put her finger on Mrs. Fiske's secret—the secret that only she knows in our time. I can see her as she sat in the circle of women listening to the confession which *Lona's* will had won from the *Consul,* and feel even now the warming glow of a triumph which indescribably irradiated her. It was the outgiving of a dynamic being, an inspirational, communicable emanation, a transcendent expression of the spirit. This, it seems to me, is acting in its highest estate, and this, I think, is the genius of Mrs. Fiske.

I told her once that her performance as *Lona* in "The Pillars of Society" was the finest acting I had ever seen. She smiled her thanks, but eyed me critically. Had I seen her play *Hedda Gabler?* No, I had not.

"Ah," she replied, "then you do not know

CPSIA information can be obtained
at www.ICGtesting.com
Printed in the USA
FFOW03n0947130416
23244FF